Journey Through the Bible

LEADER'S GUIDE

Dr. **Katheryn Pfisterer Darr**, the writer of this leader's guide, is associate professor of Hebrew Bible at Boston University School of Theology. Dr. Darr has written two books, *Far More Precious than Jewels: Perspectives on Biblical Women* and *Isaiah's Vision and the Family of God* (Westminster/John Knox, 1991, 1994). She is on the editorial board for *The New Interpreter's Bible* (Abingdon, 1994 and later) and is writing the commentary on the Book of Ezekiel for this series.

Dr. Darr is a popular speaker at United Methodist pastor and lay conferences throughout the country. She and her husband, Dr. John A. Darr, have a son, Joshua.

EZEKIEL, DANIEL, HOSEA, JOEL, AMOS, OBADIAH,
JONAH, MICAH, NAHUM, HABAKKUK,
ZEPHANIAH, HAGGAI, ZECHARIAH, MALACHI

Copyright © 1996 by Cokesbury
All rights reserved.

JOURNEY THROUGH THE BIBLE: EZEKIEL, DANIEL, HOSEA, JOEL, AMOS, OBADIAH, JONAH, MICAH, NAHUM, HABAKKUK, ZEPHANIAH, HAGGAI, ZECHARIAH, MALACHI. LEADER'S GUIDE. An official resource for The United Methodist Church prepared by the General Board of Discipleship through the Division of Church School Publications and published by Cokesbury, The United Methodist Publishing House; 201 Eighth Avenue, South; P. O. Box 801; Nashville, Tennessee 37202-0801. Printed in the United States of America.

Scripture quotations in this publication, unless otherwise indicated, are from the New Revised Standard Version of the Bible, copyrighted © 1989 by the Division of Christian Education of the National Council of the Churches of Christ in the United States of America, and are used by permission. All rights reserved.

For permission to reproduce any material in this publication, call 615-749-6421, or write to Permissions Office; 201 Eighth Avenue, South; P. O. Box 801; Nashville, Tennessee 37202-0801.

To order copies of this publication, call toll free: 800-672-1789. Call Monday through Friday, 7:00–6:30 Central Time; 5:00–4:30 Pacific Time; Saturday, 9:00–5:00. You may FAX your order to 800-445-8189. Telecommunication Device for the Deaf/Telex Telephone: 800-227-4091. Automated order system is available after office hours. Use your Cokesbury account, American Express, Visa, Discover, or MasterCard.

EDITORIAL AND DESIGN TEAM

Mary Leslie Dawson-Ramsey,
Editor

Norma L. Bates,
Assistant Editor

Linda O. Spicer,
Adult Section Assistant

Ed Wynne,
Layout Designer

Susan J. Scruggs,
Cover Design

ADMINISTRATIVE TEAM

Neil M. Alexander,
Publisher

Duane A. Ewers,
Editor of Church School Publications

Gary L. Ball-Kilbourne,
Senior Editor, Adult Publications

Art and Photo Credits: page 5, Brenda Gilliam, from *Turnabout Paul*, VBS 1995. Copyright © 1995 by Cokesbury. Reprinted by permission; page 47, (top left) © 1981 Biblical Archaeology Society, (top right) © 1991 Biblical Archaeology Society, (bottom) © 1983 Biblical Archaeology Society; page 54, from *New Ways to Tell the Old, Old Story*, by Delia Halverson. Copyright © 1992 by Abingdon Press. Used by Permission

Cokesbury

03 04 05– 10 9 8 7 6 5 4 3

THIS PUBLICATION IS PRINTED ON RECYCLED PAPER

CONTENTS

Volume 8: Ezekiel—Malachi   by Katherine Pfisterer Darr

INTRODUCTION TO THE SERIES		2
Chapter 1	"EAT THIS SCROLL"	3
Chapter 2	VISIONS OF JERUSALEM	8
Chapter 3	LOOKING BACK, LOOKING FORWARD	13
Chapter 4	ISRAEL RESTORED!	18
Chapter 5	GOD'S GLORY RETURNS: EZEKIEL'S TEMPLE VISION	23
Chapter 6	"PREPARE TO MEET YOUR GOD"	28
Chapter 7	"HOW CAN I GIVE YOU UP, EPHRAIM?"	33
Chapter 8	"BUT AS FOR ME—I AM FILLED WITH POWER"	38
Chapter 9	WHERE IS GOD'S JUSTICE?	43
Chapter 10	"A JEALOUS AND AVENGING GOD IS THE LORD"	48
Chapter 11	"I CALLED TO THE LORD OUT OF MY DISTRESS AND HE ANSWERED ME"	53
Chapter 12	"EVERYONE WHO CALLS ON THE NAME OF THE LORD SHALL BE SAVED"	58
Chapter 13.	"SEE, A DAY IS COMING FOR THE LORD"	63
MESSIANIC MOTIFS IN THE BOOK OF THE TWELVE		68
WATCHING IN THE NIGHT VISIONS: DANIEL'S APOCALYPSE AND EARLY CHRISTIAN REFLECTION OF JESUS		71
MAP: THE ANCIENT NEAR EAST		Inside back cover

Introduction to the Series

The leader's guides provided for use with JOURNEY THROUGH THE BIBLE make the following assumptions:
- adults learn in different ways:
  —by reading
  —by listening to speakers
  —by working on projects
  —by drama and roleplay
  —by using their imaginations
  —by expressing themselves creatively
  —by teaching others
- the mix of persons in your group is different from that found in any other group;
- the length of the actual time you have for teaching in a session may vary from thirty minutes to ninety minutes;
- the physical place where your class meets is not exactly like the place where any other group or class meets;
- your teaching skills, experiences, and preferences are unlike anyone else's.

We encourage you to discover and develop the ways you can best use the information and learning ideas in this leader's guide with your particular class. To get started, we suggest you try following these steps:

1. Think and pray about your individual class members. Who are they? What are they like? Why are they involved in this particular Bible study class at this particular time in their lives? What seem to be their needs? How do you think they learn best?
2. Think and pray about your class members as a group. A group takes on a character that can be different from the particular characters of the individuals who make up that group. How do your class members interact? What do they enjoy doing together? What would help them become stronger as a group?
3. Keep in mind that you are teaching this class for the sake of the class members, in order to help them increase in their faithfulness as disciples of Jesus Christ. Teachers sometimes fall prey to the danger of teaching in ways that are easiest for themselves. The best teachers accept the discomfort of taking risks and stretching their teaching skills in order to focus on what will really help the class members learn and grow in their faith.
4. Read the chapter in the study book. Read the assigned Bible passages. Read the background Bible passages, if any. Work through the Dimension 1 questions in the study book. Make a list of any items you do not understand and need to research further using such tools as Bible dictionaries, concordances, Bible atlases, and commentaries. In other words, do your homework. Be prepared with your own knowledge about the Bible passages being studied by your class.
5. Read the chapter's material in the leader's guide. You might want to begin with the "Additional Bible Helps," found at the *end* of each chapter in the leader's guide. Then look at each learning idea in the "Learning Menu."
6. Spend some time with the "Learning Menu." Notice that the "Learning Menu" is organized around Dimensions 1, 2, and 3 in the study book. Recognizing that different adults and adult classes will learn best using different teaching/learning methods, in each of the three dimensions you will find
   —at least one learning idea that is primarily discussion-based;
   —at least one learning idea that begins with a method other than discussion, but which may lead into discussion.
   Make notes about which learning ideas will work best given the unique makeup and setting of your class.
7. Decide on a lesson plan: Which learning ideas will you lead the class members through when? What materials will you need? What other preparations do you need to make? How long do you plan to spend on a particular learning idea?
8. Many experienced teachers have found that they do better if they plan more than they actually use during a class session. They also know that their class members may become frustrated if they try to do too much during a class session. In other words
   —plan more than you can actually use. That way, you have back-up learning ideas in case something does not work well or something takes much less time than you thought.
   —don't try to do everything listed in the "Learning Menu." We have intentionally offered you much more than you can use in one class session.
   —be flexible while you teach. A good lesson plan is only a guide for your use as you teach people. Keep the focus on your class members, not your lesson plan.
9. After you teach, evaluate the class session. What worked well? What did not? What did you learn from your experience of teaching that will help you plan for the next class session?

May God's Spirit be upon you as you lead your class on their *Journey Through the Bible*!

Questions or comments? Call Curric-U-Phone 1-800-251-8591.

1 "Eat This Scroll"

Ezekiel 1–5

LEARNING MENU
Based on experience with class members, select at least one option from each of the following three Dimensions. Spend approximately one-third of your session working on Dimension 1 activities. Keep in mind, however, that approximately two-thirds of class time should be spent on activities selected from Dimensions 2 and 3.

Dimension 1: What Does the Bible Say?

(A) Pray for exiles.

Our world is filled with displaced victims of economic greed, religious differences, political ambitions, and ethnic hatred. The prophet Ezekiel says nothing of the suffering and loss endured by his fellow Judeans in Babylonia. He makes no effort to console his audience and offers no prayers on their behalf.

Unlike Ezekiel, however, we can pray on behalf of contemporary exiles whose lives have been torn apart, who worry about family members far away, and whose futures seem utterly bleak.

- Join hands in a prayer circle, asking each person to contribute one or two lines to a community prayer for those suffering exile, want, fear, and loneliness around the world.

(B) Examine the map.

- Be sure that every one or two persons have access to the map of the Ancient Near East in the study book (inside back cover).
- Help them locate Judah, Jerusalem, Babylonia, Babylon, the Tigris and Euphrates Rivers, the Chebar canal/river, Nippur, and Tel-abib.
- Explain that the exiles were forced to walk the many miles from Jerusalem to Babylon. Find the way to Babylon. Using the scale of miles for the map figure the approximate distance the people had to walk into exile.

(C) Answer the questions in the study book.

- Discussion of Dimension 1 questions might evoke some of the following responses:
  1. Ezekiel begins by asserting that the four living creatures were "of human form" (1:5). Yet each has four faces—a human face in front, a lion's face on the right, the face of an ox on the left, and an eagle's face in back.

     Each of the creatures has four wings as well; with two they fly, and with two they cover their bodies. Beneath the wings are human hands. Their legs are straight, but each leg ends in the shape of a calf's hoof.
  2. The hand stretched out toward Ezekiel contains a scroll with writing on both sides. (According to conventional practice, scrolls bore writing on one side only.) Its con-

tents are words of "lamentation and mourning and woe." Ezekiel is ordered to ingest this scroll, to take God's words into his own body. Surprisingly, Ezekiel finds the scroll "sweet as honey." Does this comment reflect his agreement with its contents? Or does it simply mean that the actual eating of the object—unpleasant in prospect—is pleasing to the obedient prophet's mouth?

3. Ezekiel's life hangs in the balance as he assumes the role of Israel's sentinel. God takes with utmost seriousness the necessity that the people be warned of the consequences of their actions. So long as Ezekiel warns the wicked and the backsliding righteous that they are imperiling their very lives, he has been faithful to his task and so has saved his own life. Should he fail to do so, however, he must account for their blood.

4. Ezekiel 3:27 vexes commentators. Its most obvious meaning, however, asserts that Ezekiel will be able to speak only whenever God opens his mouth to proclaim divine oracles to the exiles. This assertion authenticates Ezekiel's claim to be God's true and reliable spokesperson.

Dimension 2: What Does the Bible Mean?

(D) Pack for exile.

- Ask your class members to sit comfortably—eyes closed, both feet on the floor. Say to them: "Close your eyes and become attuned to your own breathing. Clear your minds of concerns of the day. Leave these worries outside the classroom.

    "Imagine that you and your family must flee from your home quickly. Each of you can take only one small bundle, which must be carried every step of a long and grueling journey. There's only a little room for anything but the barest essentials. What one or two 'extras' might you and you family slip into your bundles?"

- After a few moments of reflection, ask group members to turn to a conversation partner and share the contents of their family's bundles, explaining why certain objects have been chosen.

- Still remaining in pairs, ask them to discuss these questions:
—What were some of your feelings as you were being rushed from your home?
—Did any of your items hurriedly packed into your bundle hold religious significance? What are they? What meanings does each have for you?
—If you were being exiled into a strange land in which Christian worship did not exist, how would you continue your religious practices without your church community?

- Close by reading Psalm 137.

(E) Re-create Ezekiel's vision.

- The important and vivid Scripture passages in the Bible have challenged creative people of all generations. Artists have tried to capture these visions on canvas. Musicians have been inspired to put these holy moments to music. A traditional African-American hymn, "Ezek'el Saw de Wheel," tells of Ezekiel's experience blended with Christian theology. This hymn can be found in *Songs of Zion* (Abingdon Press, 1981; No. 84). If possible ask a few class members to sing this traditional song. (You will want to ask them several days in advance, since it may be unfamiliar to them.)

- For this learning option you will need yellow, orange, and red construction paper, an assortment of markers or crayons, scissors, and glue for three or four work groups.

- Divide class members into three or four groups. Be sure each group has access to the art supplies.

- Read aloud Ezekiel's vision—Ezekiel 1:4-28.

- Ask each group to re-create Ezekiel's vision of the glory of the Lord. This daunting task becomes easier when we recall that Ezekiel's "vision" need not be reproduced with anything approaching precise detail. Strive to create an impression of God's glory as it is conveyed to you through the words of the text.

- At the end of fifteen minutes, ask the groups to display their artwork in the classroom.

- If you have been able to get some people to sing "Ezek'el Saw de Wheel," close this learning option with the hymn.

(F) Roleplay the exiles' responses.

- Before inviting your class members to participate in this learning option, share with them the contents of the "Additional Bible Helps: Why Ezekiel Spoke as He Did."

- Ask one class member to play the role of Ezekiel. Additional "actors" will be needed in the roles of men and women in Ezekiel's audience.

- During five minutes of rehearsal, "Ezekiel" should prepare to speak harsh and painful words similar to the prophet's own oracles; the "exiles" should prepare their responses of protest, self-justification, and discouragement. Given their straits, should not this prophet be speaking words of comfort and encouragement?

- After their performance, invite the actors and other class members to reflect upon the different perspectives advanced by the prophet and his audience.

- In a general class discussion raise these questions:
—How does knowing some of the historical background surrounding Ezekiel's life help you to better understand his harsh words?
—When have we as a nation heard harsh words from our national leaders?
—When have we as a denomination heard harsh or prophetic words from our religious leaders?

—When have we as a congregation heard harsh or prophetic words from our pastor and/or church leaders?
—How well are these words accepted?
—What excuses do we make for our actions?

(G) Create a sign-act.

- For this learning option you will need clay or modeling dough, paper to cover the tables, old knives or wire for cutting and shaping the clay, a variety of sticks, pieces of wood, rocks, and water (if working with clay).
- Read aloud Ezekiel 4:1-3. In this Scripture passage Yahweh orders Ezekiel to perform a sign-act.
- Ask class members, What does Ezekiel do? (Yahweh commands the prophet to take a brick that has not yet been dried in the sun and to mark it, either with the city plan of Jerusalem. What follows is a deadly serious game of soldiers. Ezekiel is to construct siege works against the "city," bringing to its walls models of the most advanced military weaponry of his day. The placing of an iron plate or griddle between the city and the prophet likely suggests the impenetrable barrier separating Jerusalem from its God and, hence, from any hope of divine intervention on its behalf.)
- Now divide class members into pairs or trios. Give each pair or trio a large piece of clay or modeling dough. Tell them to look carefully at Ezekiel's instructions from God for the sign-act. Challenge them to create a model of the sign-act found in Ezekiel 4:1-3.

(H) Interview Ezekiel, his wife, and their neighbors for the 6:00 P.M. news.

It is likely that Ezekiel's vision accounts, harsh words, and bizarre behavior stirred quite a bit of interest among members of the community of exiles.

- Ask one class member to assume the role of Ezekiel, another to play his wife, a third to conduct the interview, and several others to act as Ezekiel's neighbors.
- The interviewer should be prepared to ask Ezekiel tough questions. But because Ezekiel is unable to speak on his own, these queries must be answered by his wife and neighbors.
—How will Ezekiel's wife respond?
—What views will be represented among the public?
- After a few minutes of preparation, begin the interview process. Persons not playing roles should feel free to pose their own questions as well.
- At the end of ten minutes, ask participants to respond to the following questions:
—How did Ezekiel feel about having to remain silent?
—Was his wife inclined to defend her husband?
—Were their neighbors willing to give him the benefit of the doubt? Or were they troubled by the media's appearance?
—How would you react to such a strange personality?

Dimension 3:
What Does the Bible Mean to Us?

(I) Eat this scroll!

This learning option suggests making cinnamon "scrolls" at the beginning of your class time. If your class meets on Sunday morning this may be a welcomed treat. The recipe is as follows:

"For each [person] you will need one refrigerator biscuit, soft margarine (optional), toothpicks, two craft sticks (optional), and a mixture of cinnamon and sugar (½ cup sugar and 2 teaspoons cinnamon will be enough for one package of biscuits). Spread sheets of wax paper on a table. Have each [person] roll out a biscuit on the wax paper into a rectangle about ¼ inch thick. Spread the biscuit with margarine, if desired, and then sprinkle with the cinnamon/sugar mixture. Roll each end to the center. Insert a toothpick at the top and at the bottom to keep the biscuit closed while it bakes. (Option: Lay a craft stick on each end of the rectangle so that ends of the stick extend beyond the bottom and the top. Roll the biscuit around the sticks, meeting at the center; fasten with toothpicks.) Place on greased cookie sheet and bake in toaster oven or regular oven at 400 degrees for 5–10 minutes" (from *Turnabout Paul! VBS 1995*. Copyright © by Cokesbury. Reprinted by permission).

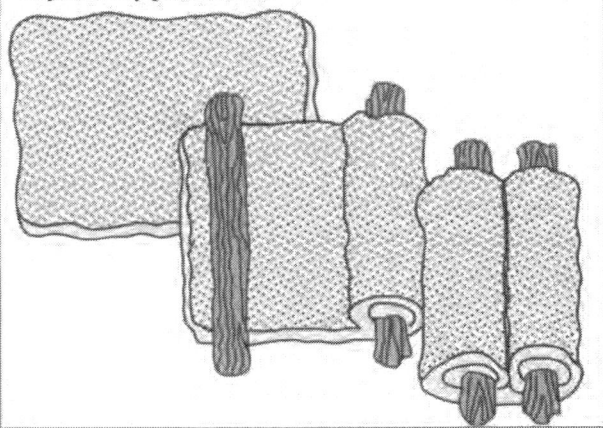

- As people gather for your class time, have the supplies for the cinnamon scrolls ready. Ask people to make the scrolls.
- Begin your session time with choices from Dimensions 1 and 2.
- As you begin discussion for this learning option ask two class members to read Ezekiel 2:1–3:5. One person can read Yahweh's words and another person can read Ezekiel's words.
- Ask for responses to this passage.

- These points may be of interest to discuss:
— Read the Scripture passage that contains Isaiah's call (Isaiah 6:1-8). Discuss the differences and similarities between Isaiah's call and Ezekiel's call.
— Read the verses following the call (Ezekiel 3:6-7). How will these words be received?
- Pass around the cinnamon scrolls. Say, "God has called each of us to be servants. Eat this scroll!"
- Ask everyone to turn to a partner and discuss what words God might be giving us today as prophets and servants. Will our words be easily received? Or will we too find an audience with a "hard forehead and a stubborn heart"?
- Close with a prayer asking for guidance as God's servants, for strength to speak words that to some are hard to hear. Ask that God's words fill you and nurture you.

(J) Join in Ezekiel's fast.

> If you or your church library has a copy of Richard J. Foster's book, *Celebration of Discipline: The Path to Spiritual Growth* (HarperSan Francisco, 1988), get it and read the fourth chapter, "The Discipline of Fasting." Or you can read the brief article on fasting at the end of this lesson. Fasting is a spiritual discipline that has declined in its practice during the last century. This resource will be especially helpful if some of your class members want to practice this discipline more fully.

- Read aloud Ezekiel 4:4-17. Note how Ezekiel's fast was not done merely for the sake of going without food. His fast was commanded by God and done in conjunction with symbolizing Israel's punishment. The act of fasting was part of Ezekiel's obedience to God's command.
- Discuss with your class members their experience of fasting.
— How many of them have ever fasted?
— What was the occasion?
— What do they remember of that experience?
— Was prayer, worship, or reflection also part of this discipline?
— Do any of them fast on a regular basis? Why, or why not?
- If class members are willing to do so, agree on a day during the coming week when they will observe Ezekiel's fast:
— eight ounces of multi-grain bread
— two-thirds a quart of water

   For health or other reasons, some participants may not be able to make such a commitment. Some class members may choose to observe Ezekiel's fast for one meal. Yet each class member may be willing to alter his or her diet somewhat for a single day as a sign of solidarity with the group. If possible, spend time in prayer and reflection during the time when you fast. However, be sure to set apart some time of your day to be in prayer while you fast.

- If restricting their diet for a day saves class members several dollars, invite them to bring this money to the next session. Participants may wish to contribute to a facility for the homeless or another local agency that addresses hunger needs.
- However, point out that the main purpose to fasting is not saving money in order to make a contribution to hungry people, but to be in closer relationship with God. Tell class members that you will have some time to talk about their fasting experience in your next class time.

(K) Sing a hymn reminiscent of Ezekiel's vision.

- For this closing option you will need enough copies of *The United Methodist Hymnal* for members to share.
- Close your time together by reading the words of the popular hymn "O Worship the King," *The United Methodist Hymnal*, 73.
- Identify ways in which the words of this hymn remind you of Ezekiel's inaugural vision of the glory of the Lord.
- Join in singing all stanzas of the hymn.

Additional Bible Helps

Why Ezekiel Spoke as He Did
(Portions of the following paragraphs appear in Katheryn Darr's article, "Ezekiel's Justifications of God: Teaching Troubling Texts," *Journal for the Study of the Old Testament* 55; 1992; pages 111–112.)

As students of Scripture, our first task is to understand, as best we are able, why the biblical authors thought and wrote as they did. Our world is far removed from Ezekiel's in many ways, and we dare not simply assume that we share his presuppositions and beliefs. In the paragraphs that follow, I attempt to articulate aspects of Ezekiel's thought. Should we agree with his assertions? We shall return to this question in Chapter 2.

Why did Ezekiel construct such harsh oracles? What were the problems that led him to speak as he did? At least four answers commend themselves to our reflection. First, Ezekiel was convinced that the events of 597 B.C. were not the end of his people's suffering. "At home in Jerusalem, and apparently in Babylon, as well, certain Yahwistic prophets promised a speedy return from exile. But Ezekiel believed that further devastation lay ahead for Judah and its inhabitants; and he sought to convince the exiles that *his* was the authentic word of the Lord.

"Secondly, Ezekiel spoke as he did because he was convinced that the coming destruction was the doing, and not the undoing, of Israel's God. In Jerusalem, the elders of Israel might be saying, 'Yahweh does not see us; the Lord has abandoned the country' (8.12), but Ezekiel rejected any notion that

JOURNEY THROUGH THE BIBLE

divine apathy [permitted] Babylonian soldiers to wreak havoc in the land, or that Jerusalem's destruction [might] signal the superiority of [the Babylonian deity] Marduk over Yahweh. He claimed historical events for [Israel's God]. He would not surrender Yahweh to history.

"Thirdly, Ezekiel's oracles reflect his conviction that what God has done, and is about to do, is not [an impulsive] act undertaken at the deity's whim, but rather is punishment for Israel's sins. If Yahweh is about to destroy the land, cities and inhabitants of Judah, it must be on account of human culpability. Israel, not God, is at fault.

"Fourthly, Ezekiel created troubling [oracles] because he believed that Yahweh was just—that the punishment was proportionate to the crime. And since the anticipated punishment was exorbitant, the sin must be grievous, indeed. On more than one occasion, Ezekiel's [fellow Judeans] are said to have challenged this view, insisting that 'the way of the Lord is unfair!' (18.25, 29; 33.17, 20). But though Ezekiel sometimes cried out at the thought of Judah's utter destruction (9.8; 11.13), he nonetheless refused to abandon his defense of divine justice."

Ezekiel had no recourse to the later notion of a "demonic power" in opposition to God. "He did not present the Babylonian attacks of 597 and 586 as part of the price one [may have to pay] for settling along [the embattled] 'Fertile Crescent' [connecting Egypt to the southwest and Mesopotamia to the east]. He wars against his fellow Judeans' complaints that Yahweh is unjust, or powerless, or apathetic. He insists that God is both in control of events, and justified in the way those events are controlled. If the God who is both just and the sovereign of history has determined to reduce Judean land and cities to uninhabited waste land, and . . . to exterminate or exile the population, then it must be because the people of Judah have sinned to such a degree that no other action is possible without violating divine justice. Ezekiel's [oracles] . . . are constructed to confirm the extent of the people's past and present sinfulness and to convince his audience that both their conviction, and their convictor, are just."

The Discipline of Fasting

"In a culture where the landscape is dotted with shrines to the Golden Arches and an assortment of Pizza Temples, fasting seems out of place, out of step with the times."

Many Christians today are searching with renewed interest for an understanding of biblical fasting. Why has fasting as a spiritual discipline fallen from practice in the last several centuries? First of all during the Middle Ages fasting developed a negative reputation as a result of ascetic and self-flagellation practices. While the movement of spirituality moved away from inward forms of exercises of discipline to more outward forms of discipline, the discipline of fasting was practiced less.

A second reason why the spiritual discipline of fasting has been on the decline is the thought that we **must** have three large meals a day, with several snacks in between to remain healthy. In reality the body can go several days without food before starvation sets in.

Fasting in Scripture

"Scripture has so much to say about fasting that we would do well to look once again at this ancient Discipline. The list of biblical personages who fasted reads like a 'Who's Who' of Scripture: Moses the lawgiver, David the king, Elijah the Prophet, Esther the queen, Daniel the seer, Anna the prophetess, Paul the apostle, Jesus Christ the incarnate Son." You may wish to look up some scriptural references to fasting:

—Leviticus 23:27; Joel 2:15; 2 Chronicles 20:1-4; Ezra 8:21-23; Matthew 6:16-18 (Sermon on the Mount).

In Matthew 9:14-17 the disciples of John question Jesus about fasting. This is perhaps the most important statement in the New Testament on whether or not Christians should fast today. Jesus made it clear that he expected his disciples to fast after he was gone. (For more Scripture references, use a concordance and look up the word *fasting*.)

Most of the Scripture references to fasting involve abstaining from all foods, solid or liquid, but not from water. Most often this type of abstinence is what is considered a fast. In most cases fasting was a private matter between the individual and God. The only public fast required in Mosaic law was on the Day of Atonement (Leviticus 23:27). This was **the day** in the Jewish calendar when the people were to be in sorrow and affliction as atonement for their sins.

Why Fast?

The purpose of fasting must always focus on God. The fast should be God-initiated and God-led. Fasting for the purpose of losing weight or getting what you want in an answer to prayer are not reasons to fast. Fasting reminds us that we are sustained by God not by food. Therefore, in the experiences of fasting we are not so much abstaining from food as we are feasting on the word of God.

Fasting is feasting! Fasting helps us keep our balance in life. How easily we begin to allow nonessentials to take precedence in our lives. How quickly we crave things we do not need until we are enslaved by them.

(Parts of this section are taken from Richard J. Foster's book *Celebration of Discipline: The Path to Spiritual Growth*, chapter 4, "The Discipline of Fasting"; HarperSan Francisco, 1988; pages 41–53.)

2 Visions of Jerusalem

Ezekiel 8–11

LEARNING MENU

Each of the activities in Dimensions 1, 2, and 3 is intended to draw class members into the biblical text, to increase their understanding of it, and to assist them in discerning its significance for their lives. Select one or more activities from Dimension 1. Remember, however, that approximately two-thirds of class time should be spent on activities taken from Dimensions 2 and 3.

Dimension 1: What Does the Bible Say?

(A) Begin by singing.

- Allow the words and tune of the hymn, "Open My Eyes, That I May See" (*The United Methodist Hymnal*, 454), to set the tone for this session.
- Recruit ahead of time someone to play the piano, or other instrument to accompany this hymn. Have this person play through the hymn once before beginning to sing. Sing all three stanzas.
- Close with this brief prayer:
  God of visions,
  As Ezekiel saw visions and experienced the power of the Spirit, open our eyes, ears, and mouths to the power of your spirit.
  Be with us today as we study and search for your word to us.
  Amen

(B) Talk about fasting.

- If any class members decided to fast this past week, be sure to include this option at the beginning of your session.
- Prior to this session gather the names of several nonprofit groups that address hunger in your community. If your congregation is already involved with such an agency, this would be an appropriate group to make any class donation to.
- Ask class members if they were able to fast.
  —Were they able to allow time for personal prayer and reflection?
  —What are their ideas about fasting as a spiritual discipline?

(C) Answer the questions in the study book.

- As always, encourage class members to read the assigned biblical texts and answer the questions in the study book *prior* to class time. In this way, they will equip themselves

8 JOURNEY THROUGH THE BIBLE

to gain the most from their time together. If class members are prepared to answer the questions, allow ten minutes for discussion; if not, allow fifteen minutes for preparation and dialogue.

- The following comments are relevant to their discussion of Dimension 1 questions:

1. The elders say, "The LORD does not see us; the LORD has forsaken the land." What do their words mean? Do they function to reassure the elders that they need not fear the consequences of their actions (which they perform, nonetheless, in the dark)? Are they an accusation: The Lord has *forsaken* the land, forcing them to rely on idols?

2. In addition to idolatry, these men are said to fill the land with "violence." This accusation is reminiscent of the charge against Noah's sinful generation (Genesis 6:11, 13). The obscure phrase, "putting the branch to their nose," likely bears the sense "provoking me to anger."

3. Seven men appear in response to Yahweh's demand for executioners. Six carry clubbing weapons of some sort. The seventh carries a scribe's kit, which scholar G. R. Driver described as follows: "A palette with a slot in which the pens were kept, and hollowed places in which the ink was put, generally two—for black and red ink" (from *Semitic Writing*; revised edition; Oxford University Press, 1954; page 86; quoted in *Ezekiel 1–20*, by Moshe Greenberg; Doubleday & Company, 1983; page 176). The seventh man is instructed to place a protective mark on the foreheads of all in Jerusalem who sigh and groan over the abominable acts being carried out in the city. The six armed men must follow him, striking dead all those whose foreheads have not received the mark.

4. Having secured the burning coals from the wheel work beneath the cherubim, the linen-clad man is to scatter them over the city of Jerusalem. Recall that Sodom and Gomorrah were destroyed in a storm of fire from heaven (Genesis 19:24).

5. Yahweh rejects their assertion that the Babylonian exiles are "far from the Lord." Although the deportees no longer reside in Jerusalem, God has been a "sanctuary" to them in the countries they have entered (not only Babylonia, but also the lands in which the exiles of the Northern Kingdom, Israel, were settled). Destruction awaits Jerusalem's inhabitants; but Yahweh will return the exiles to their land, replace their (rebellious) heart of stone with an obedient heart of flesh, and restore the covenant relationship with them. Like Jeremiah 29, then, this passage asserts that Israel's future lies with the Babylonian exiles.

Dimension 2: What Does the Bible Mean?

(D) Illustrate Ezekiel's visions of Jerusalem.

- For this learning option you will need: tape, large sheets of paper, markers and crayons, and Bibles.
- Read the information in "Additional Bible Helps: Ezekiel's Visions." This information compares and discusses the four major visions found in the Book of Ezekiel. Sharing this information as appropriate during this learning option will enhance class members' learning and prepare them for a fuller understanding as you study the other visions in future lessons.
- Tape pieces of newsprint to one wall in your classroom until you have a surface of approximately three feet by twelve feet.
- Group class members into pairs or trios. Ask each small group to select scenes from Ezekiel's visions of Jerusalem and draw them on the newsprint. You may wish to copy off the suggested vision segments from Ezekiel prior to class time on small pieces of paper. Place these papers in a box or hat for distribution. Have a representative from each group draw out a paper with its vision segment listed on the paper.
- The segments include

—Ezekiel being transported through the air from Babylonia to Jerusalem (8:3)
—The chamber of unclean animals and idols (8:10-11)
—Women weeping for Tammuz (8:14); sun worship before Yahweh's altar (8:16)
—The six executioners and the linen-clad man (9:1-11)
—The chariot throne of God's glory (10:1-15)
—The pot and its meat (11:1-7)

- At the end of ten to twelve minutes, ask persons to stand back and survey their handiwork.
- The class members may wish to keep their illustrations on the wall throughout the remainder of the study on Ezekiel.

(E) Study details from Ezekiel's visions.

- For this learning option you will need: Bibles, Bible dictionaries, commentaries on Ezekiel (if available), paper, and pencils or pens.
- Divide class members into four groups. Ask each group to select their resources from those you have gathered. Groups should select a scribe to record the results of their investigations.
- Assign each group its topic for investigation:

—**Group One**: the Canaanite goddess, Asherah
—**Group Two**: the Mesopotamian deity, Tammuz
—**Group Three**: cherubim
—**Group Four**: sun worship in Israel's ancient Near Eastern world (Begin with the article on "sun" in your Bible dictionary; then follow-up on other references listed.)
- At the end of ten minutes, ask each group's scribe to share its findings with all the class members.

(F) Investigate the phrase, "the glory of the Lord."

- For this learning option you will need Bibles, a concordance, paper, and pens or pencils. Also if your church library (or your minister's personal library) has *The Interpreter's Dictionary of the Bible*, volume E–J, look under *glory* and then under the subheadings "In the Old Testament: Divine Glory" (page 401) to gather more information about this important phrase in the Old Testament.

> **TEACHING TIP**
> Bible concordances are prepared for specific translations of the Bible. So if your class members are looking in a King James Version concordance for some references found in a New Revised Standard Version Bible, for instance, they may not find the words they are searching for. Try to match the Bibles you are working with to an appropriate concordance.

- As a whole class use a concordance to identify biblical passages outside the Book of Ezekiel in which the phrase "the glory of the Lord" appears. (Look under *glory* and read the Scripture phrases until you find those listed "g* of the Lord.")
- Divide class members into three or four groups, and assign several passages from those found in the concordance to each group.
- Group members should read their assigned passages in order to learn what they can about "the glory of the Lord."
- At the end of ten minutes, ask a reporter from each group to summarize for the entire class what it has learned. At this time you may want to add any additional information you gathered from using *The Interpreter's Dictionary of the Bible*.

(G) Take a closer look at those cherubim.

- For this learning option you will need Bibles, Bible dictionaries, paper, pencils and markers or crayons.
- Divide class members into two groups.
- Assign **Group One** Ezekiel 1:5-21 and **Group Two** Ezekiel 10:9-14.

- Ask each group to read the Scripture reference for their group and then to illustrate the description that is given.
- After several minutes working time, ask the groups to show their illustrations.
- Then ask everyone, as a whole group, to discuss these questions:
—How do the cherubim described in 10:9-14 differ from the "living creatures" described in 1:5-21? (The "living creatures" of Ezekiel 1:5-21 are called "cherubim" in 10:9-14. Apparently, each creature has four faces [though the text is unclear on this point], but the face of an ox [1:10] has been replaced by the face of a cherub. According to 1:18, each of the four wheels beside the four living creatures had eye-studded rims. Ezekiel 10:12 states, however, that the wheels had eyes on their rims and spokes. This same verse also claims that eyes fill "their entire body" and "their wings"—logically a description of the cherubim, rather than of the wheels *per se*.)
—What other descriptions are given in these verses?
—Where else in the Bible do we read of such creatures?
- If you have access to *Harper's Bible Dictionary* (1952 edition), share the information written there about cherubs and point out the photograph of a cherub in the study book (page 18).

(H) Question Ezekiel about his vision.

- Ask one member of the class to play the role of Ezekiel; invite several other class members to assume the roles of exiles seated before him in his house.
- After a period of prolonged silence, the prophet has begun to speak, describing "visions of Jerusalem" he claims to have witnessed during his mysterious translocation back to Jerusalem.
- Ask Ezekiel questions about his visions (ask other questions as they come to mind):
—Do they reflect actual events, or are they pure fantasy?
—What are the people of Jerusalem saying about us [the exiles] in our absence?
—How are our families and friends faring?
—What does it mean that the Lord's glory has departed the city?
—When can we expect to be returned to our homeland?
- The exiles may wish to speak among themselves:
—Has Ezekiel lost his mind?
—Has he distorted his words toward some religious or political end?
- At the end of ten minutes, invite both the actors and their audience to respond to what they have heard. Ask those who were not involved in the roleplay what questions they might have asked Ezekiel. Or how they would have responded to the exiles if they had been roleplaying Ezekiel.

Dimension 3: What Does the Bible Mean to Us?

(I) Create a collage.

- For this learning option you will need current newspapers, news magazines, large sheet of paper or posterboard, scissors, glue, markers, and *The United Methodist Hymnal*.
- Urban oppression and violence were, to judge from the words of Israel's and Judah's prophets, constant social problems. The majority of these prophets, like Ezekiel, place responsibility at the feet of powerful leadership groups.
- In Ezekiel 8:17, prominent Jerusalemites are accused of filling their land with violence. Ezekiel 11:1-7b asserts that the twenty-five men gathered at the east gate of the Temple have "killed many in this city, and have filled its streets with the slain." Ask a class member to read these Scripture references aloud.
- Unfortunately these images of death and destruction within the city are not unknown to us. The image of "the slain on the city streets" is timeless.
- At this point pass out the newspapers, news magazines, and other supplies. Ask class members to create a collective collage with current photographs that convey Ezekiel's images.
- After the collage is completed, ask these questions:
—How does the perspective of the biblical prophets square with your own understanding of the manifold causes of urban violence?
—What role does the contemporary church play in reducing violence?
—Does your congregation hear its own call to be an instrument for justice and peace within the world? Why or why not?
—Should a congregation be concerned about and/or involved in reducing violence within our world?
—Where and how do you start?
- Close this learning option by singing (or at least reading aloud, perhaps responsively) the hymn "All Who Love and Serve Your City," *The United Methodist Hymnal*, 433.

(J) Identify rival deities "standing" within our church sanctuaries.

- Transported to Jerusalem, Ezekiel "sees" a carved image of the goddess Asherah standing at the gateway to the Temple's inner court. This image provokes God's jealousy and resentment, since it receives the respect that belongs to God alone.
- Divide class members into small groups of three or four persons each. Ask these small groups to discuss the following questions:
—Do we bring "rival deities" with us when we enter our church sanctuary?
—What are these deities (a preoccupation with amassing material goods, concern for social standing, an "idolatrous" understanding of God that permits no new thoughts or challenges)?
—How might these rival deities affect our formal worship of God?
—What are their implications for living Christ-centered lives?
—What might be God's response to the "other gods" we carry into our sanctuaries?

(K) Consider the problem of theodicy.

- Summarize for class members the contents of the "Additional Bible Helps: The Problem of Theodicy," page 12.
- Write this definition of theodicy on a chalkboard or large piece of paper for everyone to see: Theodicy—a defense of divine justice in the face of the existence of evil.
- Note the different views of the theodicy question—
  Ezekiel—he claimed historical events for Yahweh, asserted Judah's sinfulness, and insisted that God was just—that the punishment was proportionate to the crime.
  Job—he constantly rails against the adequacy of religious language that insists upon a direct correlation between human behavior and divine response.
  Christian faith offers alternative ways of understanding God's relationship to suffering in our world.
- Encourage persons to discuss "The Problem of Theodicy" (page 12 in this guide) and its implications for our understanding of God's justice.
—Who are you most like? Ezekiel or Job?
—Is God responsible for the evils in the world? If not, then what is God's relationship to evil?
—When and under what circumstances have you struggled with the question of theodicy?
—How does our Christian faith offer alternative ways of understanding God's relationship to suffering in our world?

(L) Pray "for courage to do justice."

- Lead class members in prayer by reading aloud "For Courage to Do Justice" (*The United Methodist Hymnal*, 456):

O Lord,
open my eyes that I may see the needs of others;
open my ears that I may hear their cries;
open my heart so that they need not be without succor;
let me not be afraid to defend the weak because of the anger of the strong,
nor afraid to defend the poor because of the anger of the rich.

VISIONS OF JERUSALEM

Show me where love and hope and faith are needed,
  and use me to bring them to those places.
And so open my eyes and my ears
  that I may this coming day be able to do some
    work of peace for thee. Amen.[1]

[1] "O Lord, Open My Eyes," from *Instrument of Thy Peace*, by Alan Paton. Copyright © 1968, 1982 by the Seabury Press Inc. Reprinted by permission of HarperCollins Publishers, Inc.

Additional Bible Helps

The Problem of Theodicy
(Portions of the following section are excerpted from Katheryn Darr's article, "Ezekiel's Justifications of God: Teaching Troubling Texts"; *Journal for the Study of the Old Testament* 55 [1992]; pages 97–117.)

Ezekiel's interpretation of God's role in Jerusalem's destruction reflects the presuppositions and beliefs of his ancient Near Eastern world. Convinced that the deportation of 597 B.C. was not the end of Judah's troubles, he claimed historical events for Yahweh, asserted Judah's sinfulness, and insisted that God was just—that the punishment was proportionate to the crime. Although, on occasion, he cried out to God on the people's behalf (9:8; 11:13), his overriding concern was to defend God's justice in the face of impending devastation and crippling losses.

While understanding Ezekiel's worldview helps us better to comprehend why he spoke as he did, we dare not simply and passively accept Ezekiel's beliefs as our own. Dr. Jonathan Z. Smith offers two suggestions that can prove helpful as we ponder the problem of theodicy:

First, Smith suggests that we place texts in dialogue with each other: "*nothing must stand alone*," Smith writes. "[E]very item encountered [must have] a conversation partner, so that each may have, or be made to have, an argument with another in order that [we] may negotiate difference, evaluate, compare, and make judgments." The Book of Job makes an ideal "conversation partner" for Ezekiel, for Job constantly rails against the adequacy of religious language that insists upon a direct correlation between human behavior and divine response. And certainly, our Christian faith offers alternative ways of understanding God's relationship to suffering in our world.

Second, Smith stresses the importance of making decisions among conflicting perspectives. As Christians, we are required to think our way through difficult issues and take a stand, open to future learning though our answers must be.[2]

"And so, when students ask me [Katheryn Darr] what I think about Ezekiel's interpretation of the relationship between imperial Babylonian militarism, sixth-century Judah and the God of Israel, about his assertion that Israel's experience of exile, destruction and death at the hands of Nebuchadrezzar's troops was the punishment of a just God, proportionate and thoroughly merited, I must answer . . . I must suggest that in a world where holocausts happen, we dare not follow Ezekiel when he insists that suffering, alienation and exile are God's just punishments for sin. I do not believe that Nebuchadrezzar's destruction of a troublesome vassal was God's way of punishing the people for sinfulness. . . . In a world where holocausts happen, I must tell Ezekiel, 'No, in this, I cannot follow you.' "

[2] From " 'Narratives into Problems': The College Introductory Course and the Study of Religion" (*JAAR* 56; 1988; pages 727–39).

Ezekiel's Visions
One of the most important prophetic forms for the Book of Ezekiel is found in his visions. There are four fully elaborated visions: 1:1–3:15; 8–11; 37:1–14; and 40–48. The visions are usually introduced by a sterotyped vocabulary. By saying that "Yahweh's hand" is upon the prophet he is then removed from the everyday world and introduced into the vision given by Yahweh.

The transportation component is of interest in Ezekiel's visions. These experiences of ecstatic transportation are described in the visions as the working of the spirit. In 8:3 the spirit takes Ezekiel from his abode in exile to Jerusalem. Also in 11:1 the vision is introduced by Ezekiel being taken to the east gate of the Temple. However, in 40:1 there is no mention of the spirit in the transportation to Jerusalem. Also note the presence in 8:3 of the mysterious supernatural being who plays an active role in the vision.

While the beginnings of the visions have more set forms, the conclusions of the visions do not. Only twice is an express conclusion of the vision described. In the conclusion of the call vision the complete overwhelming of the prophet by his call is emphasized, rendering him unable to speak for a week. While on the other hand, in 11:25 Ezekiel reports immediately to his fellow exiles the nature of his vision.[3]

[3] This section is based on *Ezekiel 1: A Commentary on the Book of the Prophet Ezekiel, Chapters 1–24*, by Walther Zimmerli (Fortress Press, 1983), pages 27–28.

Due to the nature of this volume of JOURNEY THROUGH THE BIBLE, about ancient prophetic literature, additional Bible research is offered in most lessons. Since some of the historical background and traditions may be unfamiliar, taking advantage of these research options will enrich your class times together. Therefore you may need to plan ahead of time in order to find where these additional Bible resources can be obtained. Some places to look are: church library, pastor's study—with his or her permission of course—class members' libraries, college library, public library. . . .

3

Ezekiel 20:1-44

Looking Back, Looking Forward

LEARNING MENU

Based upon your knowledge of class members, their interests and needs, and the learning approaches that prove most successful, choose at least one exercise from each of the following three Dimensions. Spend approximately one-third of class time working on one or both Dimension 1 activities. Remember, however, that approximately two-thirds of class time should be spent on options in Dimensions 2 and 3.

Dimension 1: What Does the Bible Say?

(A) Begin with a hymn.

- Be sure to have enough copies of *The United Methodist Hymnal* for class members to use. If you have a pianist in your group ask him or her ahead of time to accompany class members' singing of a hymn.
- Ask class members to join in singing the familiar hymn, "A Charge to Keep I Have" (*The United Methodist Hymnal*, 413). This hymn, written by Charles Wesley in 1762, continues to challenge us to follow God's call for us.

(B) Answer the questions in the study book.

- Remind participants that they can enhance their Bible study by reading and answering these questions prior to class time. If class members have already worked through the questions in Dimension 1, spend approximately fifteen minutes sharing, discussing, and supplementing their answers.
- If they have not worked through the questions prior to class, provide a few minutes for reading Ezekiel 20:1-44, along with the questions, either individually or in teams.
- Discussion questions might evoke the following responses:
1. According to Ezekiel 20:7, Israel already was worshiping idols during its pre-Exodus years in Egypt. The Pentateuch (Genesis through Deuteronomy) tells many stories of Israel's rebelliousness in the wilderness, but it contains no charges of idolatry among the Hebrews in Egypt (the charge makes a brief appearance in Joshua 24:14).
2. In the wilderness, the Egypt-born generation of Hebrews rebels against Yahweh, refusing to observe God's statutes, rejecting God's ordinances ("by whose observance everyone shall live" (verse 13), and profaning God's sabbaths. The text makes no mention of Mount Sinai. According to the Pentateuch, however, Israel incurred responsibility for these observances as a result of the covenant forged between God and Israel at that mountain.

3. Because the children of the Egypt-born Hebrews also rejected God's statutes, ordinances, and sabbaths, Yahweh swore to "scatter them among the nations and disperse them through the countries" (verse 23). This assertion, too, comes as something of a surprise. According to Ezekiel's claim, Israel was fully deserving of exile *before* it ever entered into its land. This text stands at odds with, for example, Hosea 2:14-15, which looks back upon Israel's time in the wilderness as a period of bride-like faithfulness to God.

4. Neither Moses, Israel's venerable leader, nor Aaron, its first high priest, appear in Ezekiel's version of Israel's past, despite their prominence in the Pentateuchal materials devoted to the same period. The omission of Moses, especially, can scarcely be a matter of oversight.

5. During a second "exodus" from bondage (exile), through the "wilderness of the nations," and back to Israel's homeland, the people will undergo judgment in the wilderness. God will separate out rebels and transgressors. Although their fate is not explicitly stated, by implication they will die in the desert, as did members of the first wilderness generation.

6. The recognition formula "You shall know that I am the LORD" (verse 42; see also verse 44) bespeaks the people's eventual, thorough awareness and acceptance that Yahweh, their all-powerful God, authors and controls events.

Dimension 2: What Does the Bible Mean?

(C) Find more than one way to tell a story.

● For this learning option you will need: Bibles, commentaries on the Book of Psalms, paper, pencils or pens.
● Divide class members into two groups.(If your class is large you can work in four groups—two groups working on each Scripture passage.) Distribute the commentaries, paper, pencils or pens.

Group One: read Psalm 105:23-45
—Note how Israel's pre-Exodus period in Egypt and the years in the wilderness are treated.
—What appear to be this psalm's particular emphases?
—Does its presentation resemble the account appearing in Ezekiel 20? If not, how does it differ?

Group Two: Read Psalm 106:6-33.
—Note how Israel's pre-Exodus period in Egypt and the years in the wilderness are treated.
—What are the emphases of this psalm?
—Does its presentation resemble the account appearing in Ezekiel 20? If so, how?

● At the end of ten minutes, invite a representative from each group to present its findings to the entire class.

● Then, allow a few minutes for discussion of the following questions:
—What might account for the differences between these presentations of Israel's past?
—What questions arise when you see how differently the same event in history has been described?
● Have a general class discussion about these two Exodus accounts and how Ezekiel's account differs from the Book of Exodus account.

(D) Learn about keeping the sabbath.

For this learning option you will need several commentaries. Check your church library for reference books on the following books of the Bible: Exodus, Leviticus, Numbers, Deuteronomy, Jeremiah, Nehemiah, and Ezekiel. Each group will also need Bibles, paper, pencils or pens.

Many passages in our Hebrew Scriptures speak of the sabbath, the seventh day of the week.

According to Genesis 2:2-3, God blessed the seventh day and hallowed it because on that day, God "rested from all the work that he had done in creation" (verse 3).

The Ten Commandments include God's order that Israel "remember the sabbath day, and keep it holy" (Exodus 20:8-11). According to this passage, which refers back to the creation tradition found in Genesis 2:2-3, no Israelite shall do any work on that day, nor shall any member of his household, his livestock, or resident aliens in the towns.

● Share the above information about the sabbath as an introduction for this learning option.
● Divide class members into three groups and equip each group with Bibles, Bible commentaries for the biblical books their group is assigned, paper, and pencils or pens.
—**Group 1** texts: Exodus 35:2-3; Leviticus 23:3; Numbers 15:32-36.
—**Group 2** texts: Numbers 28:9-10; Deuteronomy 5:12-15; Jeremiah 17:21-25.
—**Group 3** texts: Exodus 31:12-17; Leviticus 26:1-2; Nehemiah 13:15-18.
● Group members should ask themselves the following questions:
—What do our texts say about the sabbath and its observance?
—What, if any, actions are expressly prohibited?
—Are some texts too general to provide much guidance in how to observe the sabbath? If so, which texts?
—Which, if any, of our texts are reminiscent of Ezekiel 20?
—How do we observe the sabbath?
—What can we learn from these Scripture passages about ways to observe the sabbath?
● At the end of ten minutes, ask one or two representatives from each group to share its findings with the class.

(E) Compare Numbers 13–14 and Ezekiel 20:23-24.

Numbers 13–14 provides a detailed account of circumstances leading to Yahweh's decision not to permit the first wilderness generation to enter the land of Canaan. (As the class leader, read these two chapters before class time. You will then be able to lead class members through this learning option by filling in some of the sections that are not suggested to be read within the class time.)

- Before class time recruit three readers to read aloud these texts: Numbers 14:13-19; Numbers 14:20-35; and Numbers 14:36-45.
- According to Numbers 13:1-24, God orders Moses to send twelve Israelites—one from each tribe—"to spy out the land of Canaan" (verse 17). After forty days, these spies return with a demoralizing report: "the people who live in the land are strong, and the towns are fortified and very large" (13:28). Only Joshua from the tribe of Ephraim and Caleb from the tribe of Judah encourage the people to take heart, trust God, and prepare to win the land. At their words, however, the Israelites threaten to stone them (14:10)!
- The Israelites have resolved to return to Egypt (14:4). Yahweh has resolved to kill the Israelites. Numbers 14:13-19 contains Moses' appeal to God not to destroy the people.
- Ask the first reader to read these verses aloud.
- Moses is able to change God's mind, but the Israelites must pay a severe penalty for their lack of trust in God.
- Ask the second reader to read Numbers 14:20-35.
- The Israelites refuse to accept God's decision. What happens when they attempt to take control of the land without Yahweh's assistance?
- Ask the third reader to read Numbers 14:36-45.
- After hearing the readings, discuss these questions:
—What *similarities* exist between Ezekiel's brief account and the lengthy story in Numbers 13–14?
—What were some of your insights while comparing these two Scripture passages?

(F) Paraphrase Scripture.

- You will need pencils and paper for class members to use.
- Ezekiel 20:40-44 describes Israel back in its land, gathered on "Mount Zion," and worshiping its God.
- Many biblical passages, including such psalms as Psalm 100, describe the joy and thanksgiving people experience as they enter the Temple in Jerusalem.
- Ezekiel, however, describes Israel's worship of God as a somber affair during which the people shall "loathe" themselves for the evils they have committed.
- Provide pencils and paper for everyone in the class. Ask them to write a paraphrase of Ezekiel 20:40-44. Encourage class members to be faithful to the meaning of the text as they understand it, to concentrate on ideas, but to put those ideas in words of their own choosing.
- At the end of eight to ten minutes, invite volunteers to share their paraphrases with everyone.
- After the paraphrases have been written, ask a class member to read aloud Psalm 100.
- Then discuss these ideas:
—What are the differences in the psalm and the Ezekiel passage?
—What emotions are conveyed in the two passages?
—Which passage would best fit your theology of the worship of God?

(G) Place yourselves in the elders' shoes.

- Ask class members to imagine that they are among the group of elders who gathered at Ezekiel's house to consult the Lord.
- Having just heard Ezekiel's negative historical retrospect, these elders have gathered outside Ezekiel's house to discuss his "extremist views."
—What might be the elders' responses to Ezekiel's version of Israel's past and his portrait of the future?
—Ask class members (as members of the group of elders gathered) to share comments they would wish to make before their peers. Would they be angry? defensive? afraid?
—How do we accept (or not accept) condemning views aimed at our practice of religion? How might Ezekiel evaluate our contemporary church and religious life?

Dimension 3: What Does the Bible Mean to Us?

(H) Deal with differences between biblical texts.

Persons sometimes use the phrase, "The Bible says . . . ," as if all of Scripture spoke with one voice.

As this lesson demonstrates, however, biblical authors who reclaimed and proclaimed Israel's traditions felt free to transform those traditions in order that they might function in new ways for later generations in their particular circumstances.

- Tell examples of these differences that you worked with in the beginning of your time together today. (This will vary depending on which learning option you chose.)
- Ask class members to turn to a partner on their right or left and to spend a few minutes discussing these questions:

—What are the implications of this insight for how we read and interpret the Bible?
—How might this insight affect our understanding of scriptural authority?
—When pastors preach from biblical texts, are they also involved in the process of reclaiming and proclaiming ancient traditions for our times? Why, or why not?
- Ask the pairs to share with the whole class some of their ideas.
—What ideas did they agree or disagree on?
—How comfortable are they with the differences in the retelling of biblical historical events?

(I) Work to further God's plan.

The elders seated before Ezekiel discover that they cannot simply decide to end Israel's relationship with Yahweh. God's will does not depend upon human decisions.
- Ask, How do we discern God's plan for us? (Scripture understood through tradition, practiced in experience, with reason applied, is the source of understanding God's will for our lives.)
   According to John Wesley's "quadrilateral," our thinking must be informed by four sources: Scripture, tradition, reason, and experience. (For a brief overview on Wesley's quadrilateral, see "Additional Bible Helps," page 17.) Both Scripture and the church teach that our thinking is enriched when it takes place within a community of believers.
- Divide class members into pairs or trios.
- Ask the small groups to discuss:
—How do you, as an individual, attempt to glimpse God's will and to live in accord with it?
—Have you heard of Wesley's quadrilateral before? How does Wesley's theory line up with your own?
—How does a congregation discern God's call for that community of faith?
- At the end of the discussion, ask participants to pledge that during the week they will renew their commitment to further God's plan in two concrete ways: one having to do with their own spiritual development, and one involving outreach to others.

(J) Close with a hymn.

Ezekiel 20 is a story of relentless human rebellion against Yahweh's purposes for the people of Israel.

No less than the Israelites of old, we may wish to reject God's will for our lives and become masters of our own fate. Ezekiel 20 insists, however, that God's plan moves forward, despite every human doubt and stubborn act.
- Join in singing the great hymn, "Make Me a Captive, Lord" (*The United Methodist Hymnal*, 412), asking God through its words to grant us that freedom that is ours only when we take our stand with God.

Additional Bible Helps

Ezekiel's Depiction of the Broken Covenant
In Ezekiel 20, the prophet constructs a story of Israel's past that functions to justify God's impending destruction of Judah and Jerusalem on account of Israel's long-lived and ongoing history of rebelliousness and sin. Those wishing to pin their hopes for deliverance on the covenant bond forged between Yahweh and Israel centuries earlier at Sinai are roundly disabused of such thoughts.

The Sinai covenant was not the only covenant bond existing between Yahweh and the people of Israel, however. Second Samuel 7 describes God's offer to enter into an unconditional covenant with King David and his offspring. Henceforth, David's descendants will always rule in Jerusalem. This unconditional covenant had implications for all the people, and not just the royal family, since God's blessings were mediated through the king to the nation as a whole.

Because Jerusalem became David's capital, and his son Solomon built a temple to Yahweh there, the city occupied a position of central importance within the Davidic covenant concept. As centuries passed, in fact, the people came to believe that Jerusalem *could not* be destroyed, since God would protect that city, and its davidic king, and its Temple against any and all foes.

In Ezekiel 16 (and also Ezekiel 23), the prophet takes on Jerusalem and the security that city symbolized for Judeans, just as he dismantles hope in Ezekiel 20. In doing so, Ezekiel adopts the literary convention of personifying cities as females. That is, throughout chapter 16, Ezekiel addresses the city as a woman, Yahweh's wife, and describes her sins through the metaphorical lens of female sexual infidelity. The result is a sustained diatribe that borders on—indeed, crosses the borders of—pornography and domestic violence. Ezekiel 16 is not for the fainthearted! Readers must remember, however, that the prophet sought to shatter any hope that Yahweh would deliver Jerusalem from Babylonia's army on the basis of "her" special relationship with God.

At the beginning of chapter 16, Ezekiel describes Jerusalem as a foundling child, the daughter of pagan parents who abandoned her immediately after her birth (verses 1-5). Yahweh sees her lying in her birth blood in a field and saves her life with the following words: "Live! and grow up like a plant of the field" (verse 6). The child matures; and the next time Yahweh passes by, the deity recognizes that she has reached marriageable age. And so God becomes her husband, providing her with the finest of garments, shoes, food, and jewelry.

Soon, however, Jerusalem forgets the husband who saved her life. She worships images of gold and silver, sacrifices Yahweh's children to these images, and plays the harlot, offering herself to passers-by at every crossroad (verses 15-22). Indeed, she behaves so lewdly that even Philistine women are shocked! Her "lovers" include Assyrians, Babylonians [Chaldea], and also Egyptians. (Here, Ezekiel is condemning Judah's foreign alliances). Unlike common prostitutes, who are paid for their services, she solicited lovers ("no one solicited you to play the whore") instead of being solicited and "gave payment, while no payment was given" to her (verse 34):

"In short, she has acted in ways that are presented as fully justifying the extravagant violence with which Yahweh, her husband, now threatens her. He will gather her former lovers and strip her naked in their presence. They, in turn, will despoil her and assemble a mob to stone her, stab her with swords, and burn her houses (the metaphor slips a bit here)" (from "Ezekiel's Justifications of God," page 103).

In its final form, Ezekiel 16 does not end with Jerusalem's mutilation and murder. Rather, the text anticipates a time when she, along with her "sisters" Sodom and Samaria will be restored (verses 46-58). In the face of this unmerited reprieve, Jerusalem will remember her former ways. Just as Ezekiel permits the worshipers of 20:40-44 no expressions of joy, so Ezekiel 16 leaves Jerusalem in a morass of shame.

Ezekiel's metaphorical depiction of Jerusalem as Yahweh's faithless wife is troubling. Certainly we cringe to discover that degradation, humiliation, physical abuse, and murder are present as means of *healing* the broken relationship between husband (Yahweh) and wife (Jerusalem), since such texts can and do have serious, life-threatening repercussions in contemporary cultures.

John Wesley's Quadrilateral
"[John] Wesley believed that the living core of the Christian faith was revealed in Scripture, illumined by tradition, vivified in personal experience, and confirmed by reason" (*The Book of Discipline of The United Methodist Church*; 1992, page 76.)

In the study of Scripture and finding its meaning for our daily life, we seek for balance. By bringing scriptural interpretation into a balance with church tradition, personal experience, and reason we are relieved of the dangers of a static and mechanical literalism in understanding Scripture.

Scripture
Scripture was always John Wesley's starting point for determining Christian truth. In conflicts of interpretation between the other sources (tradition, experience, and reason), Scripture was given ultimate authority.

Tradition
As United Methodists we are open to the power and richness of church tradition. We do not assume that we can skip forward from Old or New Testament culture to our present-day culture ignoring all the faithful living that has transpired. Christian history and its struggles have been rich. The tradition of the church has much to offer in guidance for our spiritual lives. This richness of tradition continues to grow. We are now challenged by traditions from around the world. We hear proclaimed anew the call of commitment to the poor and outcast. New voices repeat the familiar calls to justice and global peace.

Experience
Our personal experiences of God and of our lives are important to discerning the direction of our spiritual lives. John Wesley placed great emphasis on experience and was concerned that this personal side be balanced with the authority of the church and Scripture. If we do not incorporate our personal experiences, we could be trapped into a formal religion without living relationship.

"All religious experience affects all human experience; all human experience affects our understanding of religious experience" (*The Book of Discipline*, page 80).

Reason
Along with Scripture, tradition, and experience, we apply reason. We recognize that God's revelation and God's grace cannot be fully understood by our human minds. Yet we are challenged to quest for direction and understanding of God for our own lives and the lives of our communities of faith. Reason helps us to order God's revelation to us, balance it with tradition, and undergird it with Scripture.

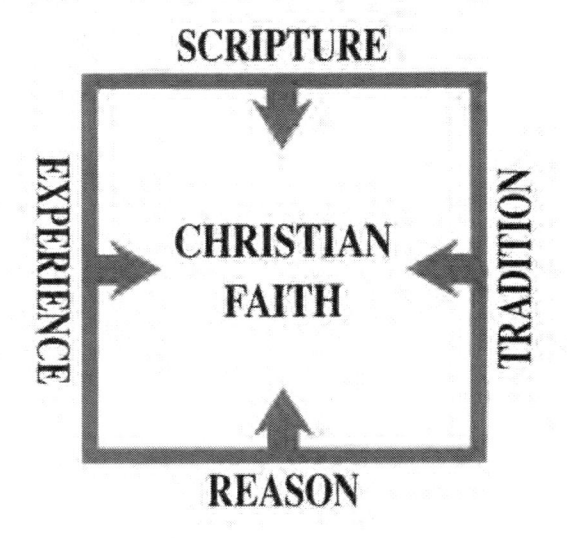

4 Israel Restored!

Ezekiel 36–37

LEARNING MENU

Based upon your knowledge of class members, their interests and needs, and the learning approaches that prove most successful, choose at least one exercise from each of the following three Dimensions. Spend approximately one-third of class time working on one or both Dimension 1 activities. Remember, however, that approximately two-thirds of class time should be spent on options in Dimensions 2 and 3.

Dimension 1: What Does the Bible Say?

(A) Join in an opening prayer of commitment to God.

Pray together the words of the great hymn, "Take My Life, and Let It Be" (*The United Methodist Hymnal*, 399). Be creative in how you pray this hymn. For example, women or a woman could read the first stanza; while the men or a man could read the second stanza; and all class members could join in the reading or singing of the last stanza.

(B) Answer the questions in the study book.

- Remind participants that they can enhance their Bible study by reading and answering these questions prior to class time. If class members have already worked through the questions in Dimension 1, spend approximately fifteen minutes sharing, discussing and supplementing their answers.
- If they have not worked through the questions prior to class time, provide a few minutes for reading Ezekiel 20:1-44, along with the questions, either individually or in teams.
- Discussion of Dimension 1 questions might include the following responses:

1. Israel's land has endured the mockery of the nations, especially Edom, becoming an object of gossip and slander. Its former habitations have been reduced to rubble; its settlements are like ghost towns. Without people to till and sow its soil, it has ceased to be fruitful and so can support neither humans nor livestock.

2. Yahweh promises to reverse these deplorable conditions. Those who have seized and gloated over Israel's land will themselves suffer insults. But the mountains of Israel shall again produce fruit. Tilled and sown, the land will be capable of sustaining a

great population, "the whole house of Israel, all of it" (36:10), as well as their livestock. Its towns will again be inhabited, its ruins rebuilt. God's good treatment of the land, Israel's inheritance, will exceed that of former times (36:11-12).

3. In chapter 36, Ezekiel stresses that God's restorative actions are not undertaken for Israel's sake. Rather, God acts in order that the divine reputation not be impeached before the nations. In Ezekiel 20, also, God's actions were influenced by concern for Yahweh's reputation among the nations. In that context, the Lord refrained from destroying idolatrous, rebellious Israel lest the nations conclude that its God was incapable of keeping the oath to bring the people out of Egypt and into the land of Canaan. Here, concern for the divine reputation results in the reestablishment of Israel in its land.

4. According to Ezekiel 37:11, the whole house of Israel is saying, "Our bones are dried up, and our hope is lost; we are cut off completely." As we shall see, it is likely that their words inspired Ezekiel's vision of the valley of dry bones (37:1-10).

5. Yahweh promises that in the future, the reunited people of God will never again defile themselves with idols and detestable things (a persistent cause of Israel's sinfulness and consequent divine wrath throughout its history) or with any other of their transgressions. Yahweh will save them from the "traps" into which they have fallen and will purify them.

6. Both David, Israel's greatest king, and Jacob, son of Isaac, grandson of Abraham, and the father of Israel's twelve tribes, are addressed as "my servant" by the Lord (Yahweh).

Dimension 2:
What Does the Bible Mean?

(C) Learn about the nation of Edom.

- Equip several research stations with Bibles, Bible dictionaries, concordances, pens or pencils, and paper. Also if possible have a large map for class members to refer to during your follow-up discussion.
- Divide class members into small groups of three or four persons each, and assign each group to a research station.
- Tell the small groups to research *Edom* and the *Edomites*.
- Some of the information they should be looking for would include:
—Where was the country located?
—What are some other Scripture references to this nation? Look those up in your Bibles and concordance.
—What were some of the land features?
—Why was this country economically important to the ancient world?
—From whom did the inhabitants of Edom descend?
—Name the encounters between the Edomites and the Israelites.
- Allow approximately ten minutes for groups to learn what they can about Edom and the Edomites.
- Ask a representative from each group to tell some of its findings to all class members.

(D) Consider the role of concern for God's reputation.

- The notion that God acts out of concern for God's own reputation may seem foreign to class members. This learning option will help you explore this concept.
- Divide class members into pairs, providing each pair with paper and pencils.
- Ask each pair to discuss and paraphrase Ezekiel's statements in chapter 36 about God restoring Israel.
- When class members have reconvened, ask for discussion of the following questions:
—Do you experience tension between a God who acts out of forgiveness and love and a God who is motivated by the reactions of others? How is that tension expressed?
—Is Ezekiel's emphasis upon God's reputation more easily understood when we remember that from the perspective of Israel's neighbors and enemies Yahweh was just one more national deity among many? Why, or why not?
—Can you remember other biblical accounts when God's reputation was of a concern for the followers of Yahweh? What are they?
—Has there ever been a time when you have "defended" God's reputation? How did you feel?

(E) Invite a rabbi to speak about Ezekiel's vision of the valley of dry bones.

If you choose this activity, you will probably wish to devote the entire class session to it. If you are not able to recruit a rabbi to speak with your class, you may be able to get a Jewish friend to come and discuss his or her tradition as it pertains to the study of Ezekiel. Be sure to discuss this speaker option with your class members. It can be very embarrassing to have a guest speaker and a very low class attendance. Also it would be especially important that class members read the Scripture passage before class time, so that they can get the most out of the speaker's visit.

- Invite a local rabbi to share with your class the significance of Ezekiel 37:1-14 for Jewish thought and experience.
—Does this text have a place in Jewish memories of the Holocaust and its aftermath?

ISRAEL RESTORED!

—How is this passage used in contemporary Jewish worship and ritual?

(F) Create collages.

- For this learning option you will need posterboard, nature magazines, markers, scissors, and glue.
- Divide class members into two groups. Supply each group with art materials.
- Ask one group to make a collage depicting the state of Israel's land prior to the fulfillment of God's promises in Ezekiel 36:1-7, 8-15.
- Ask the second group to make a collage depicting God's transformation of Israel's land (Ezekiel 36:8-15, 29-30, 33-35).
- At the end of fifteen minutes, ask each group to show its collage to the other.
- The groups may wish to display their collages in the classroom during the remainder of this study on Ezekiel.

Dimension 3:
What Does the Bible Mean to Us?

(G) Picture the dry bones of our world.

- For this learning option you will need various art supplies—paper, markers or crayons, magazines (be sure to include news magazines) and current newspapers, glue, scissors, and tape.
- Divide class members into several small groups and supply each group with art supplies.
- Recruit a class member to read aloud Ezekiel 37:1-14. This familiar passage is about the valley of dry bones. The nation of Israel seems without hope; Ezekiel's vision is a vision of hope. Even in the midst of death, God can bring hope!
- At times our nation and world may seem hopeless. Ask each small group to make a picture or a collage of the "dry bones" of our world; those places or a mindset that may seem hopeless. Ask each group to focus on one concern. After they have finished their collage or picture, ask them to write a few lines describing their concern.
- After about ten minutes ask the groups to tape their pictures on the wall for the whole class to see.
- Together compose a litany or prayer on the "dry bones" of our world. Be sure to close with words of hope. The following ideas may help you get started on this activity:

It is easy to be overwhelmed by the "dry bones" of our world:
—Hearing on the news of teenagers killing one another over designer clothes;
—Reading in newspapers of mass graves in Central Europe—new graves filled with women and children, giving a flashback to the graves dug and filled at Auschwitz and Dachau;
—Seeing homeless families huddled together at interstate ramps begging for food, money, work, warmth, and friendship;
—Telling our children that they cannot walk the four blocks home from school. We trust you to be safe, we tell them, we just cannot trust others to be kind to you;
—We weep over the dry bones of our world, as refugees wail over their loss of home and family in Eastern Europe and in Africa.
—Let us have Ezekiel's vision of hope and restoration. Let God breathe upon our world's dry bones and bring out of despair, hope, and out of death, life.

- You might want to use the litany prayer composed by class members to close this lesson or to open next week's final lesson on Ezekiel.

(H) Find your role in God's will.

> This learning option assumes that there is a level of trust among your class members. If your class is newly formed or has some new members, think carefully how you want to implement this option.

- Create a reflective mood in your classroom. You may want to play quiet music in the background. Or you may want to begin by reading a Bible passage like Psalm 134 or another general praise passage.
- Distribute paper and pencils or pens to everyone in the class.
- Ask class members to write a paragraph about their understanding of God's will. Include in this reflection what might be their role within God's will. Allow five to ten minutes for this activity.
- Ask volunteers who are willing to share their paragraphs with the class. Or you could ask each person to turn to a person on their right or left and share what they have written with that one person. Be sure to respect the fact that this type of reflection upon God's will and their call from God within God's will will be new. If an individual has difficulty with this option, she or he may want to continue this reflection at home during this week.

(I) Select meaningful objects and symbols.

- For this learning option you may choose to encourage class members to go outside or around the church building. If so, plan your total class time to allow additional time for this learning option.
- Have art supplies available if the small groups would like to draw a symbol for their Scripture. (These supplies

might include—crayons, markers, paper, glue, glitter, scissors.)
- Divide class members into three groups. Assign each group the following passages:
—**Group One**—Ezekiel 36:1-21
—**Group Two**—Ezekiel 36:22-38
—**Group Three**—Ezekiel 37
- Ask group members to select objects, images, or symbols from their verses that bear special significance for the meaning of those verses.
—Group one might, for example, select water, fruit, and fertile, well-worked soil.
—Group two might identify ruins, stones, and pastures filled with sheep.
—Group three might focus upon the rattling that accompanies the re-membering of bones to form skeletons, the sound of a rushing wind, and sticks.
- At the end of ten minutes, invite each group to show and tell about the objects and images it has selected to the whole class. Encourage them to explain the significance of each choice.

(J) Plan and participate in a closing service of worship.

- Ask class members to prepare a table containing as many of the objects, images, or symbols selected in Activity "I" as possible.
—A bowl or vase for water is probably available from the church kitchen. Participants may be able to secure stones, sticks, and soil from the church grounds. Drum sticks or other objects can be used to make rattling sounds. Group members might produce pictures of grazing sheep and other animals.
- Arrange the objects collected on the table, along with a Bible opened to some portion of Ezekiel 36–37.
- Ask participants to form a circle around the table.
- Encourage volunteers to offer prayers related to the objects. One might, for example, ask God to cleanse God's people with purifying water. A prayer of thanksgiving for fruitful soil evokes the promise of Ezekiel 36:8.
- After everyone wishing to has prayed aloud, join together in praying the Lord's Prayer.

Additional Bible Helps

Reflections on the Land
Land is one of the central themes in Hebrew Scripture. God's promise to Abram includes a land for his innumerable descendants (Genesis 12:7). When Yahweh speaks to Moses through the burning bush near Horeb, God's plan for the Hebrews includes a homeland:

"I have come down to deliver them from the Egyptians, and to bring them out of that land to a good and broad land, a land flowing with milk and honey" (Exodus 3:8).

According to the Pentateuch, the exodus from Egyptian slavery has as its immediate goal Sinai and the forging of a covenant between Yahweh and the people of Israel. But the ultimate goal is a land wherein Israel can dwell securely and enjoy the divine blessings that result from Israel's faithful adherence to the stipulations of that covenant.

In a sense, Israel's history is the story of its struggle to retain the land, for always there are other peoples wishing to seize control of it. From Israel's perspective, land is a gift from God. But the gift cannot be taken for granted. It is conditional upon the people's behavior. So long as Israel remains faithful to its God, the Lord protects its land from enemy onslaughts. If Israel ceases to be Yahweh's steadfast covenant partner, however, the gift can and will be withdrawn. In Deuteronomy 30:15-18, Moses charges the Israelites:

"See, I have set before you today life and prosperity, death and adversity. If you obey the commandments of the LORD your God that I am commanding you today, by loving the LORD your God, walking in his ways, and observing his commandments, decrees, and ordinances, then you shall live and become numerous, and the LORD your God will bless you in the land that you are entering to possess. But if your heart turns away and you do not hear, but are led astray to bow down to other gods and serve them, I declare to you today that you shall perish; you shall not live long in the land that you are crossing the Jordan to enter and possess."

Leviticus 18:25-28 states in the starkest of terms that Israel's behavior affects the land itself. This passage is preceded by a list of sexual prohibitions (Leviticus 18:6-23). According to verse 24, the former occupants of Israel's land defiled themselves by engaging in these acts. If Israel follows in their footsteps, it will share their fate:

"Do not defile yourselves in any of these ways, for by all these practices the nations I am casting out before you have defiled themselves. Thus the land became defiled; and I punished it for its iniquity, and the land vomited out its inhabitants. But you shall keep my statutes and my ordinances and commit none of these abominations, . . . otherwise the land will vomit you out for defiling it, as it vomited out the nation that was before you" (Leviticus 18:24-26, 28).

Israel has no right to defile its land gift by flouting God's statutes and ordinances.

Land brings security, but it can lead to complacency. Biblical scholar Walter Brueggemann speaks of the temptation posed by landedness:

"The central temptation of the land for Israel is that Israel will cease to remember and settle for how it is and imagine not only that it was always so but that it will always be so. Guaranteed security dulls the memory. Guaranteed satiation erodes the capacity to maintain the distance and linkage between how it was and how it is and deadens the capacity to be open to how it might yet be. Where that distance and linkage are gone, one can no longer recall a time before the gift and then we can scarcely remember that it is gift. . . .

"Settled into an eternally guaranteed situation, one scarcely knows that one is indeed addressed by the voice in history who gives gifts and makes claims. And if one is not addressed, then one does not need to answer" (*The Land*; Fortress Press, 1977; page 54).

Land poses yet another temptation—the attraction of fertility deities whose history with Israel's land predates Israel's acquisition of it. Again and again, the Hebrew Scriptures speak of Israel's attraction to deities whose devotees assert their gods' maintenance of the land in all its fullness. Should not these gods also be served? Both Israel's historiographers (the compilers and shapers of Joshua through Kings) and its prophets insist that the answer to this question is "no!" But fertility cults prove seductive. Israel looks to them to insure the ongoing fruitfulness of its land; in so doing, Israel jeopardizes the very gift it seeks to maintain.

For Ezekiel, and many other of Israel's spokespersons, failure to honor its commitments to Yahweh leads to Israel's loss of land. Moreover, the land pays a price for its inhabitants' sins. In Ezekiel 36, it lies devastated, barren, deserted, and defiled, suffering the mockery of enemies round about. God cares about the injury that the land gift endures on account of its inhabitants' sins. God also cares about damage to the divine reputation, for the nations see that Israel's land has been ruined by enemy nations, its population deported to distant lands. The nations doubtless conclude that Israel's deity proved incapable of protecting both land and people.

Nevertheless, the Book of Deuteronomy and many of Israel's prophets insist that God's ultimate plan for Israel includes secure and abundant life in its land. God will give the gift again.

Sign-Acts

A feature particularly characteristic of Ezekiel is his use of sign-acts. These acts are commanded by Yahweh. The purpose of the prophet's sign-act is to set forth in a visible action the event announced by Yahweh. This means that from the very beginning sign-acts bear importance in the total performance of the action to follow from Yahweh.

The pattern of these sign-act passages begins with an introductory divine word that commands the prophet to perform the action. This "pictorialization" by the prophet is made legitimate from the fact that it is a part of the coming divine action. The details of these actions by the prophet are of various kinds. These sign-acts vary from siege symbolism in Ezekiel 4 to the joining of two sticks in chapter 37.

As you read Ezekiel be especially attuned to the symbolism of these sign-acts. (See more in *Ezekiel 1: A Commentary of the Book of the Prophet Ezekiel, Chapters 1–24*, by Walther Zimmerli; translated by Ronald E. Clements; edited by Frank Moore Cross, Klaus Baltzer, and Leonard Jay Greenspoon; Fortress Press, 1983; pages 28–29.)

5

Ezekiel 40:1-4; 43:1-5; 47:1-12; 48:35

God's Glory Returns: Ezekiel's Temple Vision

LEARNING MENU
Keeping in mind the ways in which your class members learn best as well as their needs and interests, choose at least one learning option from each of the three Dimensions.

Dimension 1: What Does the Bible Say?

(A) Begin with a responsive reading.

- For this opening learning option you will need copies of *The United Methodist Hymnal* or enough Bibles for people to share.
- Ask a class member to lead the group in a responsive reading of Psalm 46.
- Divide class members into two sections.
- Ask them to turn to page 780 in *The United Methodist Hymnal* and to read responsively Psalm 46, with one group reading the light type and the other group reading the dark type. Try using musical Response 1 (from "A Mighty Fortress Is Our God") where the large red *R* appears in the reading.
- If hymnals are not available, ask one group to read the even-numbered verses, the other to read the odd. Conclude this opening worship by singing the first stanza of "A Mighty Fortress Is Our God."

(B) Answer the questions in the study book.

- Discussion questions might evoke the following responses:
1. Upon his arrival in Jerusalem, Ezekiel encounters a supernatural "man" (not Yahweh) with a linen cord (used for measuring long distances) and a measuring reed (for short measurements). The cord does not reappear in subsequent measurements; rather, the reed (six long cubits [= a cubit plus a handspan in length]) is used to measure the Temple area. The man tells Ezekiel to "look closely and listen attentively, and set your mind upon all that I shall show you" (verse 4), for the prophet will declare to the "house of Israel" everything he has seen in the vision.
2. Ezekiel sees "the glory of the God of Israel" approaching from the east (the same direction whence God's glory left the Temple in Ezekiel 11:22-23). Ezekiel equates this vision with that witnessed during his earlier transportation to Jerusalem (chapters 8–11) and with his first vision of Yahweh enthroned above the living creatures in Ezekiel 1:4-28. Yahweh's glory enters the Temple through its east gate; and the "spirit" lifts the prophet up, bringing him into its inner court. Yahweh's glory has filled the Temple (43:5).

3. The river begins as a tiny flow trickling out from under the threshold of the Temple toward the east. Rabbinical writings include the view (not recorded in the Book of Ezekiel) that the flow actually began at the Holy of Holies, but was too tiny to see:

"From the holy of holies to the curtain (the waters are as minute) as the feelers of the crab(?) or of the tortoise(?); from the curtain to the golden altar as the feelers of the grasshopper; from the golden altar to the threshold of the temple . . . like the warp thread; from the threshold of the temple to the outer courts (temple vestibules) like the woof thread; from there on like the outflow from the mouth of a bottle" (from *P. Seqal.* 6,50a,3; from *Kommentar zum Neuen Testament aus Talmud und Midrasch*, volume 3, by Hermann L. Strack and Paul Billerbeck; Beck, 1983; page 855; cited in *Ezekiel 2*, by Walter Zimmerli; Fortress, 1983; page 511).

4. The river transforms one of Israel's most barren and desolate areas into a veritable paradise. Ezekiel first mentions the great many trees growing on both of its banks, then reports its transformation of the Dead Sea, whose salt content (nearly 30 percent) had, since remotest antiquity, rendered it deadly to fish and other forms of aquatic life. The river's waters so purify the accursed Sea and its surroundings that all kinds of fish, "like the fish of the Great [Mediterranean] Sea," thrive; and plant life flourishes. In Ezekiel's vision, the fruit-bearing trees along its banks produce food monthly, while their leaves have healing properties.

5. Jerusalem's future name, "The LORD Is There" (*Yahweh samah*), articulates the goal toward which all of Ezekiel 40–48 moves: so conforming Israel's religious practices, leadership, and land to God's will that it will be possible for God's glory to dwell in Israel's midst forever.

Dimension 2: What Does the Bible Mean?

(C) Explore Ezekiel's "prince."

● For this learning option you will need to equip two research stations with Bibles, Bible dictionaries, commentaries on the Book of Ezekiel, paper, and pens or pencils.
● In Ezekiel 40–48, the Hebrew word translated "king" (*melek*) does not appear. Rather, Ezekiel uses the word *nasi'* to refer to Israel's ruler (who is not a priest).
● Divide class members into two groups, and assign each group to a research station.
—Assign **Group One**—Ezekiel 44:1-3; 45:7-25.
—Assign **Group Two**—Ezekiel 46:1-18; 48:21-22.
● At the end of ten minutes, invite a spokesperson from each group to share its findings with the class as a whole.

● Be sure to discuss the following questions:
—Why do you think the term *prince* was used in these passages rather than the term *king*?
—What are the prince's responsibilities? (Especially note the responsibilities in 46:1-8.)
—What limitations are placed on his power, and why?

(D) Examine Ezekiel's vision and the Zadokite priests.

Ezekiel 44:15-31 describes regulations concerning the Zadokite priests who serve at Yahweh's altar.

● Recruit two class members to read Ezekiel 44:15-31 prior to class time. (Traditionally the priests would have been men, but you do not need to limit class members' participation for this learning option.) As they read this passage ask them to prepare to be "interviewed" as a Zadokite priest from Ezekiel's vision.
● You may want to recruit a class member to serve as the interviewer or you may wish to play this role yourself. The following questions are suggested:
Let the interview begin!
—What kind of garments are the priests required to wear? What kind of cloth are they forbidden to wear, and why?
—What must the priests do with their garments when they leave the Temple? Why?
—What rules govern the priests' head and facial hair?
—When are the priests forbidden to drink wine?
—Who are the priests permitted to marry? How can you explain these marital restrictions?
—What are the priests' responsibilities?
—On whose behalf are the priests permitted to incur corpse defilement? What family member does not appear in the list?
—What is required before a priest who has incurred corpse defilement is permitted to reenter the Temple?
—What are the priests permitted to eat? What are they forbidden to eat?
—What seems to be the intent of all these restrictions?

(E) Make a collage.

● Mount newsprint on a wall in your classroom to cover a space approximately three feet by five feet.
● Provide class members with nature magazines, scissors, glue, and an assortment of markers.
● Ask a class member to read aloud Ezekiel 47:1-12.
● Then ask participants to collect pictures of various types of terrain—deserts, fertile fields, rivers and lakes, fruit trees, fish—and to supplement their pictures with drawings of their own to produce a collage depicting the dramatic transformation of Israel's wilderness and of the Dead Sea.
● Be sure to include a picture or symbol for the stream's source. Also try to include the ongoing use of this miraculous stream. (Many kinds of fish, trees that will bear fresh fruit daily, leaves that will be used for healing.)

(F) Compare Ezekiel 47:1-12 with Revelation 21:9–22:5.

Revelation 21:9–22:5 has been influenced by Ezekiel's vision, including Ezekiel 47:1-12.
- For this learning option you will need two research stations equipped with Bibles, commentaries on the books of Ezekiel and Revelation, paper, and pens or pencils. (For additional reading on the image of the sacred river found in Ezekiel, read the article in the "Additional Bible Helps" found on page 26.)
- Divide class members into two groups, and assign each group to a research station.
—Ask **Group One** to read and study Revelation 21:9-27, noting those particulars that differ from Ezekiel's Temple vision (chapters 40–42).
—Ask **Group Two** to read and study Revelation 22:1-5, noting those particulars that differ from Ezekiel 47:1-12.
- At the end of ten to fifteen minutes, invite representatives from each group to share their findings with the class as a whole.
—What similarities did you find? What differences?
—What surprised you about these differences or similarities?
—Reflect on the symbolism of water in these passages and in our use of water in the sacrament of baptism.

Dimension 3:
What Does the Bible Mean to Us?

(G) Explore the need for order and control.

- If class members are comfortable sharing personal experiences, this activity may work well. You are the best judge of what will be meaningful to your class members.
- Review the Dimension 3 section in the study book for this chapter (pages 43–44). This is a brief synopsis of Ezekiel's vision as it relates to order and control.
- Say: "We, too, often long for order in our lives. Let's reflect on when in our own lives we have longed for order and control."
- Ask participants to sit comfortably, with eyes closed, reflecting on a time in their lives when a sense of order and control has seemed unusually important.
—Was this a time when you felt out of control?
—Was this a time of transition, when so many routines were in flux?
—How was your relationship with God influenced during this time in your life?
—Is "orderliness" an important aspect of spiritual growth? Why, or why not?
- After a few moments for reflection, ask volunteers to share their thoughts with other class members.

- Also reflect on how Ezekiel must have felt about the state of the Israelite people prior to this vision. (If only there could be more religious structure and order, the people could be faithful enough to have Yahweh's glory reside in their midst.)
- How does our structure in religious life enhance our worship of God? (Order of Sunday worship, liturgical seasons of the church year [Advent, Christmas, Epiphany, Lent, Easter, Pentecost], weekly day of worship)

(H) Discover what the Lord requires.

- Ezekiel's vision presupposes that Yahweh's glory can remain in Israel's midst only as long as all aspects of its life are pure and holy. In the past, the people's abominable acts resulted in God's abandonment of the nation (Ezekiel 8–11).
- Ask class members to divide into pairs or trios for conversation.
- Ask the small groups to discuss the following questions:
—Briefly review the behavior of the Israelite people that resulted in unfaithfulness to God.
—How does the assertion that all aspects of life must be pure and holy in order to retain God's presence square with your own understanding of God's presence among humanity?
—In what sorts of contexts have you experienced the "glory of the Lord"?
—What strengths, and potential pitfalls, do you discern in Ezekiel's response to Israel's past sins?
—As Christians, where would the presence of grace fit (or not fit) into this idea of Ezekiel's?
- If you want to continue this discussion to another level you could begin a theological discussion of the relationship between grace and "good" works. For additional background reading look at the "Additional Bible Helps: Grace and Good Works" found at the end of this chapter. (Be sensitive to the various religious backgrounds that people bring to your class.)
—Share the information on "grace" and "works" with your class members.
—Ask them to remain in their pairs or trios and to discuss the relationship between grace and good works and how this relationship affects their lives.
—What is their experience in their own religious journey of the relationship between grace and good works?

(I) Study the symbolism of water.

- For this learning option you will need markers and large sheets of paper or chalkboard and chalk, Bibles, Bible dictionaries, concordances, paper, pens or pencils, and a large clear glass pitcher (or large glass) of water. Also if you choose to do the cinquain (SIHN-cane) poem portion of this learning option you may want to copy off the formula for the poem.

- Hold up the pitcher or glass of water. Ask class members how water is used. Write their answers on the large sheets of paper or on the chalkboard.
- Ask a class member to read aloud Ezekiel 47:1-12 (if you have not already done so).
- Now divide class members into small groups. Be sure each group has access to Bibles, Bible dictionaries, concordances, paper, pens, and pencils.
- Water is mentioned more frequently in Scripture than any other natural resource. Ask the small groups to research some of the different ways water is mentioned in the Bible. (The use of a Bible dictionary first to get an overview will help expedite this research.)
- Ask the small groups to report their findings to the whole group.
- Depending on the number of members in your class, decide if you want the remainder of this learning option to be done individually, in small groups, or with the whole class working together.
- Now that class members have a richer understanding of water, ask them to write a cinquain poem with water as the subject.

Poem formula:
Line 1: One-word title or subject
Line 2: Two words that describe the subject.
Line 3: Three verbs (or -ing words) or a three-word phrase about the subject.
Line 4: Four words that convey fact or feelings about the subject.
Line 5: The subject word again, or another word that refers back to the subject or title.

Example:

> Water
> Vital, wet
> Refreshing, cleansing, baptizing
> Life giving to all
> God-given

(J) Close your session by singing.

- For this closing worship time you will need copies of *The United Methodist Hymnal*. If you can recruit a pianist to accompany class members' singing, the music will enhance your closing time.
- Distribute hymnals to every two people, and invite them to join in singing "Shall We Gather at the River" (*The United Methodist Hymnal*, 723).
- At the conclusion of the hymn, recite the words from "Surely the Presence of the Lord" (*The United Methodist Hymnal*, 328) as your closing prayer.

Additional Bible Helps

Is This Vision of the Sacred River Limited to Israel?

Ezekiel and the Nations
In his commentary on Ezekiel, German biblical scholar Walther Eichrodt wrote the following words concerning Ezekiel 47:1-12, the description of the sacred river:

"The return of paradise, apparently at present limited to Palestine, is of its very nature a universal event embracing the whole world. So we may take it for granted without further demonstration that Palestine is a part that stands for the whole.... The constant formula: 'They shall know that I am Yahweh', which keeps recurring in Ezekiel, and applies to the nations as well as to Israel, therefore implies a great deal more than a mere theoretical recognition of the truth of the prophet's message. Rather, it expresses how the light of the new fellowship with God bestowed upon Israel also shines out over the Gentile world" (from *Ezekiel: A Commentary*; The Westminster Press, 1970; pages 585–586).

Eichrodt's assertion that the river's flow is but a prelude to worldwide paradise may strike a responsive chord in contemporary readers. But does it actually represent the perspective found not only in Ezekiel 47:1-12, but also in the book as a whole? Or must we conclude that Ezekiel's vision excludes, rather than includes, people and nations outside Israel's land?

"Then You Will Know That I Am the LORD [Yahweh]"
The formula, "then you [or 'they'] will know that I am the LORD [Yahweh]" appears in various forms over seventy times in the Book of Ezekiel; and its meaning is crucial to Eichrodt's interpretation of Ezekiel 47:1-12. In chapters 1–24, this phrase appears primarily in judgment oracles against Israel. Time after time, Ezekiel asserts that through depopulation (5:17; 9:5-6; 14:21), devastation (6:6; 12:20; 21:27; 33:28-29), and deportation (4:13; 6:8-10; 12:14-16; 22:15), Israel will be forced to acknowledge that Yahweh is God.

It is not enough, however, that Israel alone acknowledge God's power and control. In chapters 25–32, Ezekiel addresses various foreign nations, anticipating a time when they also will be forced to recognize Yahweh's sovereignty. They too shall experience depopulation (21:31-32; 24:13; 26:11; 27:27, 34; 28:23; 29:8, 11; 30:6, 11; 32:12, 15, 20, 22, 24-25), devastation (25:5; 26:4-5, 9-10, 12, 14, 19; 29:12a; 30:12), and deportation (29:12b; 30:23, 26), with the result that they shall "know that I am the LORD [Yahweh]."

Though Israel and the nations endure similar punishments, however, their ultimate fates will not be the same. In Ezekiel 33–48 oracles of judgment against Israel are largely

JOURNEY THROUGH THE BIBLE

replaced by promises of restoration. Yet nowhere in the book do we find a promise that other nations also will be restored. To the contrary, in oracles against foreign nations and rulers, the finality of Yahweh's punishments is emphasized. So, for example, Edom will be reduced to a "perpetual desolation" (35:9a; see also the oracle against Tyre in 26:14, 21). Yes, the nations will be forced to acknowledge Yahweh's unrivalled power and control over history, but they are nowhere promised participation in Israel's marvelous future. To the contrary, it will astonish them; and passers-by will exclaim: "This land that was desolate has become like the garden of Eden; and the waste and desolate and ruined towns are now inhabited and fortified" (36:35).

Paradise Contained

What, then, does Ezekiel say concerning the perimeters of future Eden-like conditions? If, as Eichrodt argued, "The return of paradise . . . is of its very nature a universal event embracing the whole world," then we must conclude that Ezekiel's sacred stream flows on to transform the entire world, despite the fact that the text traces its progress no further than the banks of the Dead Sea. But Eichrodt's assertion is too arbitrary. Ezekiel could surely take up the widespread notion of a transforming river, yet adapt it in ways that suited his own perspectives:

"The transformation of Israel's barren land and deadly water depicted in the book is not a foretaste of a universal return to Edenic conditions. Rather, it is a manifestation of blessing poured out upon Israel and its land which does not extend beyond Israel's borders. This depiction of 'paradise contained' is consonant with aspects of the Ezekielian perspective as a whole which we have noted—i.e., the desire that prideful and avaricious nations be forced to recognize the sovereignty and unparalleled power of Israel's God when they experience Yahweh's punishments upon them; and the conviction that Yahweh's reputation will be vindicated throughout the world when the nations witness the 're-membering' of the people of Israel in their rebuilt and rejuvenated homeland" (from "The Wall Around Paradise: Ezekielian Ideas about the Future," by Katheryn P. Darr; *Vetus Testamentum* XXXVII, 1987; page 279).

GRACE AND GOOD WORDS

"In general *grace* means favour freely shown, especially by a superior to an inferior. In the N[ew] T[estament], it denotes primarily the favour and kindness of God, freely shown to [humanity] in the incarnate life and atoning death of [Christ] (II Cor. 8.9; Phil. 2.6 ff.). . . . If as God's creatures we might reasonably expect [God] to show some favour to us, yet as sinful, ungodly creatures . . . (Rom. 5.6-10) we could deserve nothing but [God's] disfavour."

"To describe this activity of God's love as grace is to emphasize the freedom of it. For grace, as St. Augustine [church father of the fourth century] says, is not grace unless it is *gratis* [free]. . . . God's love is free in that it is unmerited. God is not moved to love us by our virtues, nor does [God] withhold [God's] love from us because of our vices."

In classical Protestant teaching we understand that we are saved "by grace alone through faith alone," apart from anything we might be able to do. Good works are a response to grace given by God. We do not do good deeds or acts of mercy in order to find favor with God. We do acts of mercy out of a response to God's grace to us (from *A Dictionary of Christian Theology*, edited by Alan Richardson; Westminster Press, 1969; pages 146, 147, 360.)

For more reading on the topic of grace and good works, borrow a dictionary of Christian theological terms from your pastor or church library.

Note to leader: Encourage class members each week to read all the suggested Scripture for the next lesson. If they are not already doing it, suggest that they use the daily Bible readings in Dimension 4 in the study book.

Point out to class members that the following chapters will not address the biblical books in the same order as they appear in the Bible. By curriculum design, these shorter prophetic books have been grouped according to similarities that they contain. For example, Nahum and Obadiah, addressed in the same chapter, are visions about Yahweh punishing their aggressors. Israel's yearnings for justice and revenge are conveyed in these two books. The books of Jonah and Daniel both are largely narrative and so are considered in one chapter.

As not to confuse your class members, point out this ordering prior to your next lesson time.

6

Amos

"Prepare to Meet Your God"

LEARNING MENU

Keeping in mind the interests and needs of class members, as well as those learning activities they most enjoy, select at least one option from each of the three following Dimensions. Spend approximately one-third of your session working on one or two Dimension 1 activities. Remember, however, that approximately two-thirds of class time should be spent on activities selected from Dimensions 2 and 3.

Dimension 1: What Does the Bible Say?

(A) Begin with a time for worship.

- You will need enough copies of *The United Methodist Hymnal* for class members to share. If possible recruit a person to teach class members and to lead them in singing the response for this psalm. The response for this reading is based on Amos 5:24.
- Turn to the Psalter reading No. 797, Psalm 76. Ask class members to divide into two groups—perhaps men and women, every other person, or another grouping. Then ask them to read the psalm responsively. Sing the musical response when the large red *R* appears at the end of each stanza.
- Pause at the end of the reading for a few moments of silence. Pray for the situations of injustice around the world. Pray that God's justice *will* roll down like the waters and that righteousness *will* flow like the streams!

(B) Answer the questions in the study book.

- Discussion of Dimension 1 questions might evoke the following observations:
1. Amos 1:3–2:5 contains oracles against Damascus (the capital of Aram, lying northeast of Israel), Gaza (an important Philistine city situated south of Israel, near the Egyptian border), Tyre (a Phoenician seaport on the eastern bank of the Mediterranean Sea), Edom (a nation whose territory was located south of the Dead Sea), the Ammonites (whose land lay east of the Dead Sea), Moab (lying between Ammon and Edom), and Judah. Amos 2:6-16, the climactic oracle of the series, addresses Israel. Many biblical scholars believe that the oracles against Tyre, Edom, and Judah were added at a later time. (See map on page 67 for these locations.)
2. In 4:6, the parallel lines, "I gave you cleanness of teeth in all your cities, / and lack of bread in all your places,"

refer to famine, an all-too-frequent result of drought and other natural disasters. In our Hebrew Scriptures, famine often appears as a consequence of human sinfulness (for example, Jeremiah 14:15-16). Verses 7-8 describe Yahweh's withholding of rain during the crucial months prior to harvest. The Lord claims to have caused rain to fall in one locale, while denying it to another. Drought, too, was seen as a divine warning or punishment. Blight, mildew, and locust swarms could destroy the fruits of an entire growing season, raising the specter of famine (verse 9); pestilence and sword took many a life; here, the deaths of strong young men are particularly in view (verse 10). All these things could be interpreted as signs of divine displeasure. The overthrow of Sodom and Gomorrah were examples of Yahweh's punishment upon greedy and inhospitable cities. According to verse 11, certain of Israel's cities have experienced their fate, becoming like a red hot brand removed from the fire.

3. Those Israelites who anticipate "the Day of the LORD" as a time when Yahweh will wreak havoc upon their nation's foes will find their expectations reversed. It will be a day of "darkness, not light, and gloom with no brightness in it" (5:20). Two "snapshots" of persons who think they have eluded death, only to be found by it, convey a sense of the inescapable nature of Yahweh's judgment (verse 19).

4. Members of Israel's upper class recline on "beds of ivory," that is, furniture decorated with elaborate ivory inlays. Their resources allow them to eat lambs from the flock (a costly indulgence, since doing so reduced the herd not only by the one lamb, but also by the number of animals that lamb could have sired or borne during its lifetime). They eat the meat of calves fattened in stalls, feast to the strains of music, drink wine from large, widemouthed bowls, and anoint themselves with the finest oils.

5. First, Amos sees the Lord God forming locusts at "the time the latter growth began to sprout," perhaps after the king had already taken the first mowing. Locusts and their larvae devoured every plant in their path. Here, they threaten the "latter growth," crucial if Israel were to survive the long drought season ahead. Second, Amos sees Yahweh summoning a shower of fire—probably a reference to the searing heat of summer, which here threatens to consume the mythical "great deep" and dry out the land. In a third vision, Amos sees Yahweh holding a plumb line next to a wall to determine its soundness. In this case, Amos does not intercede; and the reader is left to conclude that the punishment will go forward—Israel will be destroyed.

6. In 9:7a, Amos asks of Israel, "Are you not like the Ethiopians [Hebrew *Cushites*] to me? The Cushites occupied territory south of the second waterfall of the Nile. Hence, from Israel's perspective, they were an unfamiliar people living at the outer limits of the known world. The following questions place Israel's Exodus experience on par with the migrations of Philistines and Arameans. In short, these questions challenge Israel's claims both to be God's central concern and to be unique by virtue of its "salvation history" with Yahweh.

Dimension 2: What Does the Bible Mean?

(C) Interview Amos for the 6:00 news.

> An added component for this learning option that would help class members "get into their character" would be to gather old "biblical" costumes at your church. These costumes may have originally been used for Christmas or Easter plays.
>
> If finding or wearing entire costumes seems too much, try having a few props, like beards, a shepherd's staff, scarves for head coverings, available for class members to wear.

- Be sure that class members have read and are familiar with Amos 1:3–2:8. If you have not addressed this passage have a class member read the verses aloud. This section of Scripture will inform and set the stage for the Amos interview.
- Ask one class member to assume the role of Amos; ask a second person to play the role of a television reporter. Enlist several other persons to give "on the street" interviews.
- Assume that the television reporter has approached Amos immediately following his delivery of oracles against Israel's enemies and against Israel itself (1:3–2:8). He or she should ask Amos questions about his background, his decision to travel north to deliver his so-called oracles from God, his choice of subject matter, and his audacity at including an oracle against Israel in his bitter denunciation.
- In addition, the reporter should interview passers-by concerning their responses to this "radical outsider" and his sharp tongue!
- After five to eight minutes, invite others in the "audience" to pose their own questions to Amos.

(D) Make a collage.

- For this learning option you will need several sheets of newsprint or posterboard, current newspapers, news magazines, glue, scissors, construction paper, and markers.
- Secure pieces of posterboard or newsprint to a wall in your classroom until you have a surface approximately three feet by five feet.
- Invite class members to make a collage showing the social

conditions Amos found in the Northern Kingdom of Israel.
- If you have a large number in your class, you may want to divide class members into small groups. Assign each small group a section of the collage to work on. Or you could put up paper for several collages.
- Ask class members or small groups to find Scripture passages in the Book of Amos that tell of the differences between the "haves" and the "have nots." (Some example passages include: 6:1-7 and 8:4-6.)
- Be sure to include in the collage scenes of wretched poverty and scenes of rich abundance.
- Because charges of social injustice appear frequently in Israel's prophetic literature, you may wish to display your collage or collages throughout the remainder of your work in this study.
- After ten minutes or so ask class members to show their work to others in the class.

(E) Experience Israel's society from both sides.

- This activity requires that class members use all their senses in imagining themselves as part of two distinct classes in Israelite society.
- Invite persons to sit comfortably in their chairs with eyes closed while you read aloud the following excerpts from the Book of Amos. Read slowly, and pause briefly between each phrase.
- Encourage class members, in their minds, to see, feel, taste, hear, and touch the experiences of Israel's upper classes:

"... winter house ... summer house; ... houses of ivory ... great houses"; "Bring something to drink!" "... you have built houses of hewn stone ... you have planted pleasant vineyards" "... the noise of your songs ... the melody of your harps"; "... those who are at ease ... those who lie on beds of ivory, / and lounge on their couches, / and eat lambs from the flock, / and calves from the stall; / who sing idle songs to the sound of the harp, / and like David improvise on instruments of music; / who drink wine from bowls, / and anoint themselves with the finest of oils" (selections from Amos 5; 6).

Pause for a longer period of time here to make the transition from rich to poor.

- Next, encourage class members, in their minds, to see, feel, taste, hear, and touch the experiences of Israel's poor and oppressed:

"... [sell] the needy for a pair of sandals ... trample the head of the poor into the dust of the earth, ... push the afflicted out of the way ... oppress the poor, ... crush the needy, ... trample on the poor and take from them levies of grain, ... afflict the righteous, ... push aside the needy in the gate" [Recall that Israelites went to the city gate to report grievances and receive justice] "... bring to ruin the poor of the land, ... buying the poor for silver / and the needy for a pair of sandals, / and selling the sweepings of the wheat" [Israelite law required that the poor be allowed to glean in the fields, gathering the stalks of grain that the harvesters left behind.] (sections from Amos 2; 4; 5; 8).

- After several moments for silent reflection, invite group members to share their experiences of life in ancient Israel.
—What did you feel during the reflection time?
—What noises in your mind did you hear?
—How was life in ancient Israel?
—Which group of people did you feel most comfortable with?

(F) Examine an addition to the Book of Amos.

Most biblical scholars agree that Amos 9:11-15 was added to the book long after Amos's lifetime—indeed, only after the Southern Kingdom of Judah had been defeated by the Babylonians in 587 B.C.

- For this learning option you will need to equip two or more research stations (depending on the size of your class) with Amos commentaries, Bibles, paper, pens or pencils.
- Divide class members into two or three groups, and direct each group to a work station.
- Invite each group to learn what it can about Amos 9:11-15. The following questions may help direct the research:
—What features of the text suggest that it was written after 587 B.C.?
—What is the significance of the reference to Edom in verse 12?
—How does this text respond to Amos's descriptions of Yahweh's judgment against Israel?
—Who is included in the reference to "my people Israel" (verse 14)?
- After ten minutes, invite each group to report several of its findings with the class as a whole. Which, if any verses or sections, surprised class members during their research?

Dimension 3: What Does the Bible Mean to Us?

(G) Put yourself in Amaziah's place.

- In this learning option you will be discussing the article at the end of the leader's guide to this lesson, "Put Yourself in ... Amaziah's Place!" [am-uh-ZIGH-uh], page 32. You or someone in the group should either read or summarize the essay for class members.
- Decide which is best for your group: to divide into smaller

groups or to invite discussion with all class members. The size and nature of your group will instruct you here.
- Ask volunteers to share their thoughts about this essay, which invites them to fill the shoes of Amos's opponent at Bethel.
—Does this article cast a different light on Amos's activity? If so, how do you view Amos now?
—How might you have responded to Amos were you in Amaziah's position?
—How are our churches sometimes like Amaziah? (Pleased about maintaining our own buildings and programming and not reaching beyond our own church walls?)
—How are Amos's words calling us today?

(H) Identify a modern-day Amos and Amaziah.

- If you select this activity, you will need to read or summarize "Put Yourself in . . . Amaziah's Place!" (page 32) prior to the discussion.
- Ask class members to reflect on individuals in today's public or private spheres who remind them of Amos and of Amaziah. Who are they?
—Has the church a need for both types of leaders? Why, or why not?
—Can both types of leaders function together, or are they inevitably at odds with one another?
—Can there be a balance of ministry to ourselves and beyond ourselves? Or is that type of rationale not taking seriously the needs of the poor? Discuss the reasons for your answer.

(I) Discuss God's call to you.

According to Amos 1:1 and 7:14, Amos was "among the shepherds of Tekoa" and "a dresser of sycamore trees." Taken at face value, these biographical notices seem to suggest that Amos was a "man of the land" in Judah. Scholars caution, however, that these brief ascriptions cannot simply be taken as evidence that Amos was himself poor. To the contrary, he may have had considerable means. Certainly his writings strongly suggest that he was highly literate, a poet of considerable stature, and conversant with Israel's religious and wisdom traditions.

Amos states in 7:15 that Yahweh "took me from following the flock, and the LORD said to me, 'Go, prophesy to my people Israel.' " This verse suggests that Amos's "prophetic career" began abruptly, that Yahweh plucked him from his daily life and thrust his commission upon him.

- Divide class members into pairs or trios for conversation groupings. Ask the small groups to consider the following questions:
—Can you imagine yourself as suddenly sent by God to perform so difficult and unpopular a task in another land? Why, or why not?
—How might you go about attempting to confirm that your experience of God's call was authentic?
—Would you have the courage to respond to God's call?
—How might you set about to meet such a challenge? Would you take Amos's abrupt appearances and shocking statements at populous places as a model?
—What other approaches might you consider?
- Ask class members to reflect aloud about these and other questions that may have surfaced during their small group discussions.

(J) Review some major words from the "minor prophets."

The traditional label "minor prophets" (which refers to the books written by Hosea, Joel, Amos, Obadiah, Jonah, Micah, Nahum, Habakkuk, Zephaniah, Haggai, Zechariah, and Malachi) can be misleading. This label does not mean less important than the "major prophets" (Isaiah, Jeremiah, Ezekiel, and Daniel); rather the label grew out of a description of the length of their books. Some of the most familiar prophetic Scripture passages come from these "minor prophets."

- In this learning option you will be reading and researching modern writings (books, speeches, lectionary) that use the words of these prophets to support their point or theme.

Since an important theme for many of the prophets is social justice, people of faith who have written and spoken out concerning these issues often quote these prophets. The following books and speeches are some examples you will want to gather before class time. Do not limit your references to these, but search out some of your own:
—*Rich Christians in an Age of Hunger: A Biblical Study*, by Ronald J. Sider; Intervarsity Press, 1978;
—*Living More with Less*, by Doris Janzen Longacre; Herald Press, 1984;
—*The Mustard Seed Conspiracy*, by Tom Sine; Word Books, 1981;
—Dr. Martin Luther King, Jr.'s speech "I See the Promised Land" (1968) and his "Letter From Birmingham City Jail" (1963). (Dr. King's speeches can be found in numerous sources.)

Your public or church library will probably have other books appropriate for this activity. Also try to obtain a copy of the lectionary. (The lectionary is a list of recommended Scripture passages to be used in worship. These suggested readings follow the seasons of the Christian year and try to address the important themes in the Bible. Your pastor or church library will probably have a copy.)

- Divide class members into three small groups. Ask the groups to review the resources you have and to look at the context in which the prophets' words are quoted. The following questions may help in starting a discussion:

—In your opinion did the author stay true to the prophet's original concern?

—How do these words speak to you and/or your congregation?

—Can you think of other times these prophetic words have been used? When and how?

—Looking at the lectionary, when are Scriptures from these prophetic books used?

—Do you remember a worship service when one of these passages was used? When? How?

(K) Close with a hymn.

- Close your time together by singing "When the Church of Jesus," *The United Methodist Hymnal*, 592. If possible plan for someone to accompany your group while singing this hymn. Or if you have a soloist in your class, recruit him or her (ahead of time certainly) to sing this hymn for your closing worship.
- Like the prophet Amos, this hymn challenges us in that we cannot become complacent in our churches thinking that all is well because we are well. We proclaim with this hymn that our pious devotion should not soar us above the world needs, but forge our Christian worship into Christian deeds.
- If you do not have enough hymnals for all class members to be able to see the hymn, ask three people to each read one stanza for your closing time.

Additional Bible Helps

Put Yourself in . . . Amaziah's Place!

As readers, we are likely to empathize with Amos, God's spokesperson for social justice and righteousness, and to oppose those he condemned. As noted in this lesson, however, the reaction of Amaziah, priest of Bethel, to Amos's prophecy concerning the death of King Jeroboam was remarkably tolerant.

Given our tendency to side with Amos, it may seem strange to put ourselves in Amaziah's place. But consider this scenario: You are the chair of the pastor/parish relations committee at First Church Bethel. Things are going well. Attendance is the best it's been in years. Giving is at an all-time high. Why, the last stewardship campaign was so successful that today, the average church member tithes *more* than ten percent! There's still a great deal to be done, of course; while so many have so much, too many do not have enough. The poor are, indeed, always with us. So programs must be organized in order to coax money from the rich and redistribute it to the poor, the widowed, the orphans. Yes, there's a great deal to be done. Still, things are going well.

Who's this? Amos, a southerner who's ripe and ready to tell us how we're failing? Doesn't he know that it's bad enough to be criticized by home folk? Criticism from uppity outsiders is intolerable! What's he offering—a helping hand, or the overthrow of our nation? Does he conduct himself with proper decorum when he enters the royal religious site, the king's sanctuary, a temple of the kingdom? He does not! Instead Amos places himself in the most visible spot and proceeds to utter what can only be described as pure blasphemy: "Jeroboam shall die by the sword, / and Israel must go into exile away from his land" (Amos 7:11). He is announcing that the long anticipated "Day of the Lord" will be a time when Yahweh fights against, rather than on behalf of, us. He claims that our iniquities exceed those of our most hated, heathen enemies—Moabites, Ammonites, and the like. Worst of all, Amos dares compare Israel's most sacred tradition about the exodus from Egypt to the stories of Philistine and Syrian migrations—as if Israel were just another nation in Yahweh's eyes.

Amos's words ran roughshod over many of Israel's most cherished beliefs. Surely, his presence horrified Amaziah. Perhaps if the accusations had been expressed tactfully, in discrete surroundings, Amaziah could have given them a more objective hearing. Perhaps he would even have agreed with some of Amos's criticism and formed a committee to investigate how the community might be improved on the basis of Amos's critique. Such would have been his way. Amaziah, after all, was the official priest of a royal sanctuary. He was fair-minded, capable, prudent, a well-integrated and respected member of his society. Of course he could be critical of his community! But Amaziah undoubtedly understood that controversial messages must be handled delicately. He knew the importance of balancing social criticism with social expectation. He knew that, sometimes, God's people must walk a fine line between divine demands and the all-too-human need for stability and expediency.

Under the circumstances, Amaziah could not allow Amos to continue his blasphemous diatribe there, within the king's sanctuary. And so he spoke to Amos; and all things considered, his words showed remarkable restraint: "O seer, go, flee away to the land of Judah, earn your bread there, and prophesy there." Go home, Amos! Take the beam out of your own eye, Amos! But don't disrupt life here. Your sort has no place at the king's sanctuary. If changes must be made, I'll make them; and I won't alienate half the kingdom while I do it.

But Amos, a peripheral prophet, is not interested in maintaining a delicate balance between the status quo and divine demands. He plays a destabilizing, rather than a validating, role in the religious lives of his Northern Israelite contemporaries. Amos blows in, blows off, and blows out. And the Bible gives no indication that he kicked up a similar fuss in his own backyard.

7 Hosea

"How Can I Give You Up, Ephraim?"

LEARNING MENU
Each of the activities in Dimensions 1, 2, and 3 is intended to draw class members into the biblical text, to increase their understanding of it, and to assist them in discerning its significance for their lives. Select one or two activities from Dimension 1. Remember, however, that approximately two-thirds of class time should be spent on activities taken from Dimensions 2 and 3.

Dimension 1: What Does the Bible Say?

(A) Open with a responsive reading.

The themes of divine mercy, trust in God, the folly of worshiping false gods, and offering empty sacrifices are strongly present in the Book of Hosea. The responsive reading of Psalm 40:1-11 conveys these same themes.
- For this opening worship time you will need enough copies of *The United Methodist Hymnal* for class members to share.
- Divide class members into two groups. Ask everyone to turn to No. 774 in the hymnal and begin the reading. One group should read the verses appearing in regular type, the other those verses appearing in boldface type. Everyone joins in reading (or singing) the response, marked *R*.

(B) Stage a dramatic reading of Hosea 1 and 2.

- Recruit your readers as the class members gather for the session to begin. All readers will need a Bible; the members of the chorus will need to read from the same version of the Bible.
- In order to read Hosea 1–2 dramatically, you will need to assign the following roles and verses to participants:
—Chorus (three or more class members)—1:1-11
—Yahweh—2:1-4, 6, 8-11, 13-23
—Israel (the wife)—2:5, 7, 12
- You may want to pose these general questions to class members at the conclusion of the reading:
—What information were we given about the family of Hosea?
—What are the charges levied against Israel?
—Is redemption possible for Israel?

(C) Answer the questions in the study book.

- Remind people that they can enhance their class experience by reading the Book of Hosea and answering the questions in their study books prior to the session.

- If class members have already worked through the questions in Dimension 1, spend ten to fifteen minutes sharing, discussing, and supplementing their answers.
- If class members have not yet worked through the questions, allow a few minutes for reading them, along with the relevant biblical texts, either individually or in teams.
- Discussion of Dimension 1 questions might include the following responses:

1. Hosea's marriage to Gomer, his unfaithful wife, functions as a metaphor to illumine Yahweh's relationship with unfaithful Israel. Both ancient Near Eastern marriage and Yahweh's covenant with Israel required absolute fidelity of the subordinate partner.
2. According to 4:1-3, the people of Israel have failed to give God their *'emet* ("faithfulness") and *hesed* ("steadfast devotion"). They lack "knowledge of God," that is, "knowledge of [God's] teachings as the source of a harmonious community life within Israel" (from *Hosea*, by Hans Walter Wolff, edited by Paul D. Hanson, translated by Gary Stansell; Fortress, 1974; page 67); and as a result, they engage in swearing, lying, stealing, adultery, and murder.
3. Although Israel's prayer in 6:1-3 sounds sincere, Yahweh judges it to be superficial and short-lived, "like the dew that goes away early" (verse 4). Again, Yahweh calls for genuine *hesed* ("steadfast devotion") and knowledge of God.
4. According to Hosea 9:7-9, the people of Israel insult and attack God's prophets. The prophet assumes the role of God's watchman over Israel, whose job it is to warn the people of approaching danger; but the people are too corrupt to hear and to heed his words.
5. Yahweh promises to heal and to love Israel, to revive and to make fruitful the nation, tending it and protecting it from dangers. These verses are filled with plant and flower imagery; indeed, the people of Israel's future are likened to lilies, the forests of Lebanon, olive trees, gardens, and vines.

Dimension 2: What Does the Bible Mean?

(D) Learn more about the Northern Kingdom's kings.

- For this learning option you will need to equip three research stations with: Bibles, Bible dictionaries, concordances, paper, and pencils or pens.
- Also you may want to prepare a large timeline that class members can refer to during the course of this study. If so, you will need two pieces of posterboard or several large sheets of newsprint, masking tape, and markers. Draw a line down the center of the posterboard to begin your timeline.
- Divide class members into three groups, and assign each group to a research table.
—Assign **Group One** to learn what it can about Jeroboam II and his son, Zechariah (not to be confused with the biblical prophet of the same name).
—Assign **Group Two** to investigate Shallum and Menahem.
—Assign **Group Three** to research Pekahiah and Pekah.
- At the end of ten minutes, invite a representative from each group to report its findings to the whole class. At this time a representative from each small group can write on the large class timeline the name, date, and a short interesting fact or two about the kings from their research.

(E) What's in a name?

> An additional resource you may want to have available for this learning option is a book on names. These popular books are often times used when selecting a name for a baby. For example, Luke, bringer of light; or Amy, beloved.

- In this learning option you will be exploring the concept of message names and how these were used in the Old Testament.
- Names are very important and often help shape who we are and who we become. (Perhaps one of the most difficult tasks of new parents is to choose what to name their newborn.) To begin this learning option go around the room and ask people to share some brief information about their own personal name. Have a book of names available in case some of your class members do not know any information about their name and would like to find out what it might mean.
- After this discussion recruit a class member to read Hosea 1:2-9 aloud.
- Then ask class members these questions:
—What are the names of Hosea's wife and their three children?
—What is the meaning of each child's name? (Hosea married "Gomer, the daughter of Diblaim." The children's names are Jezreel ["God sows"], Lo-ruhamah ["not pitied"], and Lo-ammi ["not my people"].)
—What other prophets gave their children message names? Or what other Old Testament people gave their children names that God commanded?

(F) Make an accusation.

- Provide paper and a pencil or pen for each class member and have several commentaries on Hosea available for reference.

34 JOURNEY THROUGH THE BIBLE

- Divide class members into pairs or trios. Ask one of them to read aloud Hosea 7.
- Ask the pairs or trios to select one or two of Hosea's accusations against Israel and to write a paraphrase of the accusation or accusations. They can use the commentaries on Hosea for reference on chapter 7.
- Ask participants to think creatively about how Hosea's audiences might have responded to his accusations. Recall that people tend to justify their actions, rather than admitting that charges lodged against them are true.
- When class members have completed these two tasks, ask them to share their findings with persons sitting next to them, or with the class as a whole.

(G) Investigate the Canaanite deity, Baal.

- Divide class members into two groups.
- Assign **Group One** to a research table equipped with Bible dictionaries (the volume with the "B" entries), paper, and pencils or pens. Ask this group to learn what it can about the Canaanite deity, Baal.
- Assign **Group Two** to a research table equipped with Bibles and a Bible concordance. Ask this group to look up biblical passages referring to Baal and record what they learn from those passages.
- At the end of ten minutes ask Group One, and then Group Two, to report its findings to the entire class.

(H) Compare Israel's idolatry and Yahweh's fidelity.

- For this learning option you will need several large pieces of newsprint or posterboard, markers, and tape. Also you will need a commentary on the Book of Hosea.
- Hosea 13:1-3 describes Israel's idolatry and its consequences. Verses 4-8 describe Yahweh's past fidelity and present rage.
- Divide a piece of newsprint into two columns. On the left side, record words and phrases descriptive of Israel's idolatry. Consult a commentary concerning the charge in verse 2, "People are kissing calves!"
- On the right side, record words and phrases descriptive of Yahweh's past provision for the Israelites. What kind of imagery dominates the description of Yahweh's punishment in verses 7-8?
- Recruit a class member to read aloud chapter 13 in Hosea. Read only a few verses at a time; then pause, and enter on the newsprint chart examples of Israel's idolatry or Yahweh's fidelity.
- After class members have worked through this chapter, discuss these questions with them:
—What images are most vivid to you? Read them aloud to class members.
—Does Yahweh's rage surprise you?

Dimension 3:
What Does the Bible Mean to Us?

(I) Discuss God, human nature, and relationships.

- Divide class members into conversation groups of three to five persons. If they have not read the first three chapters of Hosea, give them time to do so. Ask them, in light of their reading of Hosea 1–3, to consider the following questions:
—What do these chapters tell us about God?
—How does the metaphor of individual characters (a husband and a wife) representing the situation of Yahweh with Israel strike you? (The "children" are thought to represent the individual Israelites over and against the corporate nation [the wife].)
—What do these chapters tell us about human nature?
—What do these chapters tell us about our relationship with God?
—What do these passages tell us about our relationships with, and responsibilities to, persons in our communities?
- At the end of ten minutes, ask one person from each group to give a summary of that group's responses to one of the five questions posed, insuring that each of the five questions is addressed by one of the groups.

(J) Consider how Israel's social ills resemble our own.

Hosea identified a number of problems in the Northern Kingdom's (Israelite) society of his day: violence, deceit, injustice, idolatry, arrogance, and indulgences.

These conditions strongly suggest that the relationship between God and the people of Israel had been broken, because the latter disregarded Yahweh's teachings.

Alien though Hosea's prophecies sometimes seem, certain critiques of his nation seem applicable to our own as well.

- Ask one member of the group to play the role of Hosea, God's spokesperson. Give this person several minutes to scan the Book of Hosea and to select quotations and themes of judgment that are appropriate to our society.
- Ask several other persons to play the role of leaders in our society. (You need not attach specific names to these persons).
- Provide five minutes for dialogue between "Hosea" and representatives of our own, twentieth-century situation. What might Hosea say to them? How might they respond? (Note how naturally rationale comes to defend one's own situation.)
- At the end of five minutes, ask other class members to assume the roles of Hosea and of modern-day leaders. Allow the dialogue to continue for another five minutes.

- At the end of ten minutes, ask group members to share their thoughts about these dialogues.
- Also invite discussion on the following questions:
— What prophetic words of Hosea apply to your church? to our society?
— How can we as people of faith prepare ourselves to better hear prophetic words of judgment?
— As Christians through Christ our sins have been forgiven. Grace abounds. Are we then still under prophetic judgments such as Hosea's? Why, or why not?

(K) Look at Yahweh as a parent.

- This learning option will take a look at the passage found in Hosea 11 that adopts a parent image for Yahweh. You will need Bibles, concordances, Hosea commentaries, and Bible dictionaries as resources for your groups.
- Divide class members into two conversation groups. Recruit a class member to read aloud Hosea 11:1-4.
- Hosea often refers to Israel as Ephraim. Ask each group to research *Ephraim*.
— Who was the "original" Ephraim?
— What are some of the different references to Ephraim in the Old Testament?
— Why do you think Hosea used this name to refer to Israel?
— What metaphor in 11:1-4 describes Yahweh's relationship to Israel? (Yahweh adopts parent-child imagery to describe God's tender, nurturing care for Israel in its infancy.)
— Do these nurturing images of Yahweh surprise you? Why, or why not?
— What are your responses to these images?
- After the groups have had enough time to do their research and discuss their findings, ask a group representative to report its insights to the whole class.
- A general question to raise at the end of this learning option would be, "How do these tender images of Yahweh balance with Yahweh's rage that Hosea presents in chapter 13?"

(L) Close with a time for reflection.

Hosea leaves us with many images; most of the images are without hope. This closing reflection time tries to pull these thoughts together and offer hope.

- Ask class members to get comfortable, perhaps to close their eyes. Ask them to try to clear their minds and to listen to the words read.
- Read aloud Hosea 13:14.
- Then share these thoughts with class members. (This meditation is adapted and reprinted by permission from *Places Along the Way: Meditations on the Journey of Faith*, by Martin Marty, copyright © 1994 by Augsburg Fortress.)

"*Sheol*. This is the shadow land, the depths with no exit, the utterly depressing place. . . . Sheol was the netherworld, the dark underground, the world's pit. Dead and departed spirits were supposed to dwell there. Who praised God in Sheol?

"Hosea, the prophet who spoke of Sheol, knew something about disappointment and despair over human existence. . . . [Hosea tells us of] God's frequently frustrated goal of being faithful to the faithless Israel. The response of Hosea was to pronounce judgment, judgment, judgment."

How have we been faithless to God? When have we chosen our path as opposed to choosing God's path? When have we been "kissing calves" (13:2b) and worshiping idols of our culture and not God?

"We could not endure the image of Sheol in Hosea's words of judgment if it were not for the last chapter of his prophecy. There he answers yes to God's questions about rescue from Sheol. Yes, God shall ransom people. Yes, God shall redeem them from death and offer life!"

- Close by reading aloud Hosea 14:1-7

Additional Bible Helps

Marriage, Prostitution, and Adultery in Ancient Israel
As we begin reading the Book of Hosea we are immediately embroiled in family fact, symbol, and metaphor. We learn of Hosea's wife of questionable reputation. We then read of Yahweh's faithless wife, Israel. The roles and ways of women are important in understanding more fully the message of Hosea. The following information hopefully will bring more understanding of these complex cultural roles of women of the ancient world.

(The following paragraphs are excerpted, with some emendation, from Chapter 3, "The Ways Women Are," in Katheryn P. Darr's book, *Isaiah's Vision and the Family of God* [Westminster/John Knox Press, 1994; pages 95, 97, 115–121].)

Marriage
Hosea 1–3 reveals that in ancient Israelite society, the emotive ties joining husbands and wives were both powerful and complex, encompassing tender nurture/provision and severe discipline, immense love and explosive rage. Marriage was an important legal and economic transaction with broad implications for a family's survival, status, and day-to-day life. But it was also an artificial bond:

"As opposed to the natural and biological ties of siblings, or parents and children, that of man and wife is artificial, created and defined by the customs of a given community. The legal codes of the Bible and Mesopotamia reflect this peculiarity of marriage with their numerous statutes regulating and defining this more frail institution" (from "The Background for the Metaphor of Covenant as Marriage in the Hebrew Bible"; Ph.D. dissertation by E. J. Adler; University of California at Berkeley, 1989; pages 66–7).

J. Galambush has compared marriage in biblical Israelite society to ancient Near Eastern suzerain-vassal treaties (i.e., political treaties forged between superior [the suzerain] and inferior [the vassal] entities:

"Israelite marriage was, like vassaldom, a relationship of mutual obligation between two parties, one (the husband) superior and the other (the wife) inferior in terms of their legal status. As in a treaty agreement, the husband was required to protect the wife . . ., and the wife was to obey the husband, and to refrain from sexual relationships with other men. The husband, like the suzerain, was free of any such obligation of exclusivity" (from *Jerusalem in the Book of Ezekiel: The City as Yahweh's Wife*; Scholars Press, 1992; page 33).

Prostitution

References to prostitution appear in biblical and extra-biblical texts from the ancient Near East. From such references, we learn something of how and why women were forced into prostitution; and we also gain a sense of how prostitutes were regarded within their societies.

Ancient Near Eastern women became prostitutes for reasons as old as the profession itself. "Then, as throughout history," scholar Rivkah Harris observes, "girls became prostitutes as a result of poverty, war, and male violence. They came from the ranks of the poor, captives of war, and foreigners" (from "Independent Women in Ancient Mesopotamia?" in *Women's Earliest Records: From Ancient Egypt and Western Asia*, edited by B. S. Lesko; Scholars Press, 1989; page 149).

While prostitution was not illegal, social attitudes toward prostitutes were at best ambiguous and at worst extremely negative. On the one hand, they were "important in the leisure activities of . . . men" (from "Images of Women in the Gilgamesh Epic," in *Lingering Over Words*, edited by T. Abusch and others; Scholars Press, 1990; page 222). On the other hand, so-called "wanton women" were "abnormal" and "dangerous" because they lived outside the circle of home and family and threatened its security (from "Non-Royal Women in the Late Babylonian Period: A Survey," by Amelie Kuhrt, in *Women's Earliest Records from Ancient Egypt and Western Asia*; page 238).

Adultery

In ancient Israel's patrilineal society, land passed from father to son(s). Female sexual infidelity threaten patrilineal inheritance patterns, for a married woman's illicit liaison with a man other than her husband could result in land being passed to an illegitimate heir. Moreover, the promiscuous wife was guilty of dispensing what was not legally hers to control, shaming and angering both her husband and his family. If, as Carol Newsom observes, woman is the "essential thread" joining the pieces of patriarchy's social fabric, she also "indicates the seams where the fabric is subject to tears" (from "Women and the Discourse of Patriarchal Wisdom: A Study of Proverbs 1–9"; in *Gender and Difference in Ancient Israel*, edited by Peggy L. Day; Fortress, 1989; page 155).

In describing adultery, the biblical authors not only used the term *n'p*, "to commit adultery," but also *znh*, "to commit fornication, be a harlot." "The use of *znh* rather than *n'p*," Phyllis Bird observes, "serves to emphasize promiscuity rather than infidelity, 'wantonness' rather than violation of marriage contract or covenant. The connotations [are] of repeated, habitual, or characteristic behavior. . . . The metaphorical use of *znh* invokes two familiar and linguistically identified images of dishonor in Israelite culture, the common prostitute and the promiscuous daughter or wife" (from " 'To Play the Harlot': An Inquiry into an Old Testament Metaphor," in *Gender and Difference in Ancient Israel*; pages 80, 89). Moreover, E. J. Adler adds, *znh* identifies a motive (economic profit), and applies to the adulteress the prostitute's associations with treachery and callousness ("The Background for the Metaphor of Covenant as Marriage in the Hebrew Bible"; pages 311–14).

8 Micah

"But As for Me— I Am Filled With Power"

LEARNING MENU

Keeping in mind the interests and needs of your class, as well as those learning activities they most enjoy, select at least one learning segment from each of the three following Dimensions. Dimension 1 focuses your class upon the biblical texts themselves—the first and most crucial step! Spend approximately one-third of your session working on one or more Dimension 1 activities. Remember, however, that approximately two-thirds of class time should be spent on Dimensions 2 and 3.

Dimension 1: What Does the Bible Say?

(A) Begin with a hymn.

"What Does the Lord Require," *The United Methodist Hymnal*, 441, is based on the words of Micah 6:6-8. Albert F. Bayly wrote this hymn in 1949. Early in Bayly's hymn-writing career he wrote a series of hymns to interpret the message of each of the Hebrew prophets in the Old Testament, "viewing them in the light of the climax and fulfillment of the Old Testament revelation in the coming of Christ" (from *Companion to The United Methodist Hymnal*, edited by Carlton Young; The United Methodist Publishing House, 1993; page 689).

- If you have a pianist among your class members, before class time ask him or her to accompany class members in the singing of this hymn. If you choose not to use the piano accompaniment, you may decide to ask four different class members each to read one stanza of the hymn and all the class members to join in on the last part of each stanza, "Do justly; love mercy; walk humbly with your God."
- You will need copies of *The United Methodist Hymnal* for this opening learning option. Invite class members to join in singing or reading responsively all four stanzas of "What Does the Lord Require," number 441.
- When you have finished singing or reading this hymn, ask class members what they think is meant by the phrases "do justly," "love mercy," and "walk humbly with your God."

(B) Answer the questions in the study book.

- Discussion of Dimension 1 questions might raise the following comments:
1. Micah summons all peoples—indeed, the entire earth—to witness Yahweh's disputation with Israel on account of its sinfulness. In 6:1, mountains and hills serve as wit-

nesses to yet another divine controversy with Israel (6:1-8). Both passages are examples of the lawsuit genre frequently used by Israel's prophets. In such lawsuits, Yahweh assumes the roles of both plaintiff and judge.

2. Micah's audience responds to his words by urging him to silence. His dire messages are, they claim, utterly inappropriate and false. Micah rebukes his chastisers. People such as they would only respond to prophets proclaiming "empty falsehoods." Mockingly, he claims that such prophets would say, "I will preach to you of wine and strong drink" (2:11). Intoxicating words may seem to hold reality at bay, but of course do not. In 3:6, Yahweh charges the prophets with giving pleasant messages to those who meet their fees, while declaring "war" against those unwilling or unable to pay. As punishment, God will withdraw from them any vision or revelation, leaving them disgraced.

3. While Micah 3:12 proclaims that Zion will be utterly destroyed, "plowed as a field," 4:1-4 describes Zion's future *beyond* judgment, when the city and its temple become pre-eminent among the nations, and peoples of the world stream to "the mountain of the LORD" to receive Yahweh's instruction. The shift in content and tone between these two passages could scarcely be more abrupt or dramatic.

4. According to Micah 6:6-8, Yahweh does not require endless sacrifices. Rather, the Lord requires that Israel
—Do justice—justice, we shall see, is a quality Micah claims to be sorely lacking among Israel's leaders;
—Love faithfulness (kindness)—acts of steadfast love toward one's neighbors likewise find no expression in Judah's society, where exploitation and oppression reign;
—Walk humbly with your God—the term "humbly" is at home within Israel's wisdom traditions, where it describes appropriate conduct according to God's will.

Dimension 2: What Does the Bible Mean?

(C) Draw a picture.

Theophany (thee-OF-uh-nee) is a manifestation of God and its devastating, awesome effects upon creation.

- For this learning option you will need drawing paper, crayons or markers, and pencils.
- Divide class members into three or four small groups, depending on the size of your class. Distribute art supplies to each group.
- Read aloud Micah 1:3-4. Then ask each small group to draw a picture of this scene.
—What will be the effects upon nature when Yahweh comes down to judge Jacob/the house of Israel (1:3-4)?
(This passage contains dramatic depictions of Yahweh striding across the high places of the earth, as mountains melt beneath the Lord's feet and valleys burst open. Descriptions of Yahweh's awesome effects upon nature are characteristic of biblical theophanies.)

- After the small groups have finished, ask someone from each group to show its drawing and to tell which images were important to the group.
- Ask these questions to the whole class for a general discussion:
—Why do you think these dramatic images of Yahweh were used in Hebrew writings?
—From some of your other studies can you think of other examples of theophanies? What are they?

(D) Experience a lament.

- Ask participants to sit quietly, their feet on the floor, arms relaxed, and eyes closed.
- Tell them to visualize the images and experience the emotions in Micah 7:1-6 as you read the text aloud in a slow, solemn voice.
- When you have finished reading, give class members several minutes to reflect silently on what they have seen with their mind's eye. After about three minutes, ask them slowly to open their eyes.
- Allow ten minutes for class discussion of what they have experienced. Depending on the trust level and size of your class, you may want to ask class members to turn to the person on their right or left and discuss what they experienced. If your class is small and your members feel comfortable with one another, you might choose to have a full-class discussion on the responses to the biblical reflection experience.

(E) Prepare a mural of Zion.

- Tape pieces of newsprint to one wall in your classroom until you have a surface of approximately three feet by five feet. Divide the surface into two halves.
- You will also need a variety of markers, magazines (including sports and news magazines), scissors, and glue.
- Divide class members into two groups.
- Ask **Group One** to draw Zion as it appears in Micah 3:9-12.
- Ask **Group Two** to work with Micah 4:1-4. Each group will use one half of the newsprint mural area.
- At the end of fifteen minutes, ask participants to stand back and to talk about their handiwork.
—Can one group guess which images spoke to the other group?
—How can these images be referring to the same city?
—Where have you heard or seen 4:3 used in other contexts?
- Class members may wish to keep their illustrations on the wall for a week or two.

(F) Explore God's relationship with Israel.

- For this learning option you will need Bibles, commentaries on the Book of Micah, paper, and pens or pencils.
- Divide class members into three groups. Provide each group with the above materials.
- Assign each group a portion of Micah 6–7:
— **Group One**—Micah 6:1-5
— **Group Two**—Micah 7:8-10
— **Group Three**—Micah 7:14-20
- Ask a representative from each group to read its verses aloud. Ask each group to study and reflect on the passage without the use of the commentary first, then to refer to the commentary for additional insights.
- After the reading, each group should ask the following questions of its text:
— What do these verses tell us about God?
— What do these verses tell us about human beings?
— What do these verses tell us about our relationship with God?
— What, according to the text, is God's will for human communities?
— What images in the texts are familiar? Unfamiliar?
— What new information or insights were you able to gain from using a commentary? Do you agree or disagree with the commentator's view of the passage?
- At the end of ten minutes, invite a representative from each group to share several of its findings with the class as a whole.

(G) Evaluate Micah's use of female imagery.

FEMALE IMAGERY

Metaphors invite us to perceive something through terms that are suggestive of something else. Micah's female imagery describes the tribulation of the times and the end of such tribulation. The book personifies Jerusalem as a woman (daughter Zion) who endures the mockery of enemies, but who also stands resolutely in her faith in Yahweh.

- For this learning option you will need Bibles (a variety of translations would be good), commentaries on the Book of Micah (or one commentary that could be passed around), paper, pens or pencils.
- Divide class members into two groups.
- Assign the following passages to each group:
— **Group One**—Micah 4:8, 9-13
— **Group Two**—Micah 5:2-5; 7:8-10

Additional information for Group Two about the beginning of its passage:

Micah 5:2 begins with an address to Bethlehem of Ephrathah. In some biblical texts, Ephrathah is simply equated with Bethlehem. In others, the former appears as a region distinct from the latter; in any event, the terms are closely related in this and other biblical texts (see Ruth 1:2). Most significant for this text is the fact that both proper nouns are traditionally associated with King David, whose father Jesse was from Bethlehem (1 Samuel 16:1, 18) and is called an Ephrathite from Bethlehem in 1 Samuel 17:12. In proclaiming that from Bethlehem of Ephrathah "shall come forth for me [Yahweh] one who is to rule in Israel," the text stops short of identifying the future king as a direct descendant of David, but associates him nonetheless with Israel's "ancient" and most famous king, the recipient of Yahweh's covenant (2 Samuel 7).

- Ask each group to address the following questions:
— When and in what biblical book have you found female imagery for Jerusalem before?
— What stereotypical roles, experiences, and ideas about women are highlighted in Micah's female imagery (example: vulnerability, the pain of childbirth)?
— What kind of response do you have when you find female imagery in the Bible?
- At the end of about ten minutes, invite a spokesperson from each group to report on its findings to the entire class.

(H) Tour the wealthy and impoverished districts of Jerusalem.

- This learning option will help unleash the creativity of class members.
- Ask one class member to assume the role of Micah. Ask another person to play the role of his companion, the beneficiary of Micah's tour of wealthy and impoverished districts of Jerusalem. Ask four to five other class members to play, on the one hand, wealthy Judeans, and on the other, members of the impoverished class. (The same persons should play both roles.)
- From your study of the Book of Micah you will have gleaned what the overall social conditions of Jerusalem were in Micah's day. However, if you want a few Scripture passages to review prior to this roleplay, the following verses give more of the social context: 2:1-5; 3:1-3; 6:9-16; 7:1-6.
- Provide space at the front of the classroom for the "tour" to take place.
- As Micah and his companion walk through the wealthy district, Micah should offer appropriate comments,

including responses to his companion's questions. They may stop from time to time to question rich passers-by about their view of Jerusalem and its future.
- As Micah and his companion walk the streets of impoverished districts, they should continue their conversation, pausing occasionally to speak to poor passers-by, including farmers who have come to the city for the first time. Ask these town folk about the conditions of their city and about their treatment from the leaders and rulers.
- At the end of ten to fifteen minutes, allow time for all class members to discuss what they have seen and heard.

Dimension 3: What Does the Bible Mean to Us?

(I) Identify God's moral mandates.

- For this learning option you will need several pieces of newsprint or posterboard, markers, and tape.
- Invite class members to listen carefully as you read Micah 3:9-11; 6:6-8, 10-16.
- Recruit two class members to be "scribes." Record on newsprint or posterboard a list of God's moral mandates in a collage fashion (not in straight columns, but at different angles). Some are stated positively, others emerge from criticisms of what people are doing. Select two colors to use for recording these mandates. Write all the positive moral mandates with one color and all the criticisms with another color.
- Raise these questions when the listings are finished:
—Are there more positive mandates or more criticisms?
—Is one type more general than the other?
—Are these moral mandates the same as those we hold to be true in our society? Why, or why not?
—How does contemporary American society succeed or fail in living up to God's standards?

(J) Compose a communal lament.

In Micah 7:1-6, a speaker describes the vulnerability and hopelessness he is experiencing as part of a society in which the faithful are victims and evildoers prevail.

Every day, newspapers, television, and magazines report social injustices in our own nation and in the world.

In our faith communities, we can lament in the face of catastrophes that seem so senseless, or that vividly illustrate the consequences of human greed, oppression, and deceit.
- For this learning option you will need sheets of newsprint or posterboard, markers, tape, and a current newspaper.
- Divide class members into three or four groups. Each group needs newsprint and markers. The newspaper can be available in case one of the groups has difficulty thinking of a current social injustice situation.

- Ask each group to identify a particular crisis, at home or in the world that they wish to lament in prayer to God.
- Ask each group to compose a lament concerning that crisis. Their laments may or may not be loosely patterned on Micah 7:1-6. Groups may wish to reflect upon God's role in the midst of suffering in ways that differ from ancient Israel's ways. And, of course, their laments may well reflect the centrality of Christ for the Christian faith.
- At the end of ten minutes, invite each group to share its lament with the class as a whole.
- Taking turns, each group could lead the class in praying its lament.

(K) Conclude with hope.

- Ask your class members to reflect upon the Book of Micah:
—What are some of the themes that have arisen?
—Is God pleased with Israel? Why, or why not?
—According to the evidence given to us by Micah and other prophets, is God's wrath justified? Explain.
- Read aloud Micah 7:18-20.
- Ask class members this question:
—What is the theme of Micah 7:18-20? (Micah 7:18-20 emphasizes Yahweh's forgiveness of human iniquity, not because persons deserve such forgiveness, but because God is compassionate and faithful to God's promises.)

(L) End with prayer and praise.

- For this closing worship option you will need copies of *The United Methodist Hymnal* and Bibles. Ask class members to open their Bibles to Micah 6:6-8. Distribute copies of the hymnal before the quiet prayer time begins.
- Try to recruit ahead of time someone to accompany your class's singing the hymn "Behold a Broken World," number 426. If this is not possible, ask six members to each read a stanza of the hymn. Note that this hymn by Timothy Dudley-Smith is based on Micah 4:1-4.
- Arrange the chairs in your classroom into a circle.
- Ask persons to pray silently about some aspect of Micah's message that speaks to a need for spiritual growth and action in their own lives. After several minutes, read aloud Micah 7:18-20.
- Ask them to pray silently about a time when they have trusted in God, despite uncertainty and fear. After several minutes, read aloud Micah 7:7.
- Allow class members several minutes to offer a silent prayer of consecration to God's will for their lives. Then, lead them in reciting or reading Micah 6:6-8. End with "Amen."
- Close this worship time by singing or reading the hymn "Behold a Broken World."

Additional Bible Helps:

External Piety Does Not Suffice

To judge from certain prophetic passages in our Hebrew Scripture, one would think that God rejects the very sacrificial system that, according to the Pentateuch (Genesis–Deuteronomy), was given to Israel by Yahweh in the course of the covenant-making experience at Sinai. Recall, for example, Amos's deeply ironic summons to Israel's sanctuaries:

> "Come to Bethel—and transgress;
>   to Gilgal—and multiply transgression;
> bring your sacrifices every morning,
>   your tithes every three days;
> bring a thank offering of leavened bread,
>   and proclaim freewill offerings, publish them;
> for so you love to do, O people of Israel!
>   says the Lord GOD." (Amos 4:4-5)

Isaiah 1:13-15 presents the offering of sacrifices in the worst possible light:

> "Bringing offerings is futile;
>   incense is an abomination to me.
> New moon and sabbath and calling of convocation—
>   I cannot endure solemn assemblies with
>   iniquity.
> Your new moons and your appointed festivals
>   my soul hates;
> they have become a burden to me,
>   I am weary of bearing them.
> When you stretch out your hands,
>   I will hide my eyes from you;
> even though you make many prayers,
>   I will not listen;
>   your hands are full of blood."

And, as we have seen, Micah 6:6-8 disavows any notion that sacrifices alone are an appropriate response to the question of what Yahweh requires.

Close, contextual reading of these and other prophetic passages reveals, however, that ancient Israel's sacrificial system *per se* was not the actual target of such prophetic critiques. Rather, the prophets condemned acts of sacrifice that were, in their view, empty examples of external pietism. These acts bear no relation to internal attitudes—genuine repentance and willingness henceforth to "walking humbly" with God, sincere thanksgiving leading to the desire to share one's blessings with others. Bustling religious sites were not necessary indications of sincere and vibrant faith in God, the prophets insisted. Wealthy folk who gave what their prosperity allowed them comfortably to part with, persons who brought their sacrifices with the blood of their victims on their hands (literally or figuratively), people who gave for show, in order to enhance personal and professional reputations—such "worshipers" perverted the meanings and functions of ancient Israel's religious practices; and the prophets asserted that God would have none of it. Moreover, the priests in charge of religious rituals, including sacrifice, were themselves corrupt.

This theme continues in the New Testament writings of the earliest Christians. In Mark 11:15-19, Jesus drives out those businessmen (and women?) who have set up shop in proximity to the Temple in Jerusalem, "who were selling and those who were buying in the temple, and he overturned the tables of the money changers and the seats of those who sold doves," charging that "a house of prayer" had become a "den of robbers" (see also Matthew 21:12-13; Luke 19:45-48; John 2:13-17). Marketplace mentality had no place, Jesus asserted, where prayer and sacrifice were to take place. Elsewhere (Mark 12:41-44; Luke 21:1-4), Jesus spotlights for his disciples a poor widow who placed two copper coins in the Temple treasury, as wealthy people were depositing large sums. "Truly I tell you," the Jesus of Mark's Gospel proclaims, "this poor widow has put in more than all those who are contributing to the treasury. For all of them have contributed out of their abundance; but she out of her poverty has put in everything she had, all she had to live on" (Mark 12:43-44).

Abundant sacrifices and sacrificial giving are not the same. The prophets agree that what God requires of human beings ultimately has to do not with external acts of piety, but with the heart. Nowhere is this tenet of our faith expressed more profoundly than in Micah 6:6-8.

9

Habakkuk; Zephaniah

Where Is God's Justice?

LEARNING MENU

Each of the activities in Dimensions 1, 2, and 3 is intended to draw class members into the biblical text, to increase their understanding of it, and to assist them in discerning its significance for their lives. Select one or two activities from Dimension 1. Remember, however, that approximately two-thirds of class time should be spent on activities chosen from Dimensions 2 and 3.

Dimension 1: What Does the Bible Say?

(A) Begin with a prayer of petition.

- For this opening worship option you will need copies of *The United Methodist Hymnal*, a large piece of posterboard, a sheet of newsprint or a chalkboard, marker or chalk, and tape (if not using a chalkboard). Before class time copy the refrain below so that the whole class can read it. The response (R) is from Zephaniah 3:15:

(R) The LORD has taken away the judgments against you,
    he has turned away your enemies.
The king of Israel, the LORD, is in your midst;
    you shall fear disaster no more.

- Divide the class into two groups. Distribute copies of *The United Methodist Hymnal*. Ask class members to turn in the Psalter to No. 809, Psalm 90. (NOTE: the reading continues on page 810.)
—Ask **Group One** to read those verses of Psalm 90 printed in regular type.
—Ask **Group Two** to read those verses printed in bold type.
—Tell the class members about the refrain substitution taken from Zephaniah 3:15 listed on the board. Use the Zephaniah refrain when the large, red *R* is noted in the reading.

(B) Answer the questions in the study book.

- Discussion of Dimension 1 questions might evoke the following observations:

Zephaniah

1. The opening verses of the Book of Zephaniah encompass all of God's creation—humans and animals—asserting that Yahweh will "sweep away" everything from the face of the earth.

    The sins Zephaniah condemns Judah and Jerusalem for are the sins of unfaithfulness.

2. Zephaniah 3:14-20, a text infused with joy, urges daughter Zion/Israel to sing aloud, rejoice, and exult, for Yahweh has dropped charges against her and removed her

foes. Her king, the Lord, dwells in her midst; and as a result, she need no longer fear disaster. Verse 17 describes Yahweh as a victorious warrior who rejoices over her—indeed, exults over her with loud singing, just as Zion is called to sing and exult in verse 14. God shall gather all the people whom Zion embodies, including society's weakest members, bring them home, restore their fortunes, and cause them to be praised among the nations of the earth.

Habakkuk
1. Habakkuk cries out because he sees no end to suffering and violence. Continually, he witnesses destruction and brutality. Neither Yahweh's Torah, nor instruction (the responsibility of Israel's priests), nor justice can prevail under such circumstances. The wicked imperil the righteous.

   Yahweh responds, as we shall see, by pointing to the Chaldeans (that is, the Babylonians) whom God claims to be rousing—a "fierce and impetuous," "dread and fearsome" people. It seems that Yahweh intends to use the Babylonians as an instrument against those whom Habakkuk indicts in verses 2-4.
2. The concluding verses of the Book of Habakkuk are a statement of trust in God that persists despite present barrenness of field and flock. The poet rejoices "in the God of my salvation," who is his strength (verses 18-19).

Dimension 2: What Does the Bible Mean?

(C) Investigate geographical references in Zephaniah.

- For this learning option each class member needs to have access to a Bible and the study book.
- Depending on the number of class members you may need to work in pairs or trios in order for each person to see the map located in the study book. Or you can make copies of the map found on the inside back cover of this leader's guide.
- Ask this general question of your class members:
—What cities and nations are the objects of prophetic attack in Zephaniah 2?
- Then share the following information during the discussion: Chapter 2 of Zephaniah proclaims that on the "great day of the LORD," God shall sweep away the inhabitants of four principal Philistine cities—Gaza, Ashkelon, Ashdod, and Ekron—as well as the people of Crete (the Cherethites, also Philistines); Canaan, land of the Philistines; and the Philistine-controlled seacoasts. These verses (2:4-6) reflect the ancient enmity between Israel and the Philistines, one of many "sea peoples" whose skill in iron work afforded them an advantage in warfare. The territory under Philistine control shall become pasture land for "the remnant of the house of Judah" (verse 7).

Turning east, the prophet condemns Moab and Ammon, also traditional enemies of Israel. According to biblical tradition, these two nations' origins could be traced back to the daughters of Lot who, following the destruction of Sodom and Gomorrah, plied their father with wine and through him became pregnant with Moab (MOH-ab), ancestor of the Moabites, and with Ben-ammi (ben-AM-igh), ancestor of the Ammonites (Genesis 19:30-38). In light of this tradition, the claim that "Moab shall become like Sodom and the Ammonites like Gomorrah" (verse 9) takes on added significance.

Zephaniah also proclaims the deaths of the Ethiopians (Hebrew "Cushites"), a people living south of Egypt and hence at the furthest stretch of the known world. Finally, Zephaniah turns north to proclaim the destruction of Assyria and its capital, Nineveh, whose army approached Israel and Judah from the northwest along the route called the "Fertile Crescent."

- Now ask class members to turn to the map of "The Ancient Near East." The map is found on the inside back cover of the study book and of this leader's guide.
- Assist group members in locating Gaza, Ashkelon, Ashdod, Ekron, Crete, Ammon, Moab, the land of the Ethiopians, the "Fertile Crescent," Assyria, and Nineveh.

(D) Share Lady Zion's experiences.

- Ask class members to sit quietly with eyes closed.
- Explain that the Book of Zephaniah, like a number of other prophetic collections, personifies Jerusalem as a woman in 3:14-17.
- Read aloud 3:1-7, in which Jerusalem is not so personified. Pause. Then read aloud 3:14-17.
- When you have finished reading, allow a few moments for reflection. Then ask for responses to the following questions:
—How does the poetic technique of personifying Jerusalem as a woman affect your understanding of the city's experience in 3:14-17?
—Can you think of other biblical examples when personification is used? What are they?
—Can you think of contemporary literary or cultural examples where personification is used?

(E) Investigate images and idols.

- For this learning option you will need Bibles, Bible dictionaries, Bible commentaries, paper, and pens or pencils. Note information in "Additional Bible Helps" about images and idols (page 47).
- Divide class members into three or four small groups.

Supply them with Bibles, paper, pens, commentaries, and Bible dictionaries.

- Ask each group to begin its research on idols by reading Habakkuk 2:18-20.
— How does the author of Habakkuk 2:18-19 seek to belittle idols? (The peoples of Israel's ancient Near Eastern world likely regarded images made by human beings as representations of gods and goddesses, rather than as the deities themselves. Biblical arguments against images such as appear in Habakkuk 2:18-19 [see also Isaiah 40:18-20; 41:7; 46:5-7] make no distinction between images and the deities they represented. Hence, they mock idols [that is, other deities], because they have no breath in them and cannot speak, move, or instruct.)
- Using the information found in a Bible dictionary discuss the following questions:
— What were the differences between images and idols for the ancient Near Eastern people?
— When is it thought that the Hebrew people began their struggles against idolatry?
— Is it thought that idols both of women and of men were used in the ancient Near Eastern world?
— Have statues representing Yahweh been found?
— Using references given in commentaries or a Bible dictionary look up at least two other Old Testament references to idols. Share this information in your group.
— Did conflict with idol worshiping stop with the Old Testament accounts? Look up one reference to idols found in the New Testament.
— Do we as Christians have difficulty with idol worship today? If so how?

(F) Look for the divine warrior.

Metaphors invite us to perceive something through terms that are suggestive of something else. Habakkuk's divine warrior metaphor depicts Yahweh's past, mighty acts on Israel's behalf.

- Provide each group with Bibles, concordances, Bible dictionaries, a commentary on Habakkuk, paper, copies of the study book, and pencils or pens.
- Divide class members into three groups and supply them with the above resources.
- Ask each group to read Habakkuk 3:3-16. Then address the following questions:
— Have you previously encountered divine warrior imagery in the Bible? Where?
— What stereotypical roles, experiences, and ideas about warriors and warfare are highlighted in Habakkuk's victory song?.
— What is the significance of references to Teman, Mount Paran, Cushan, and Midian?
- At the end of ten minutes, invite a spokesperson from each group to report its findings to the entire class.

(G) Conduct a press conference with Habakkuk.

- To help in your own preparation for this learning option you may want to read the article, "The Nations as God's Instruments" found in the "Additional Bible Helps," page 46. Include information from this article when appropriate during this learning option.
- Ask one class member to assume the role of Habakkuk. All other persons should function as reporters.
- Based on their reading of Habakkuk 1–3, members of the press should ask Habakkuk questions, which he (or she) is prepared to answer on the basis of his (or her) own understanding of the book.
- Possible questions include the following:
— What emboldened you to ask God the questions appearing in 1:2-3?
— Do you believe that Yahweh uses one nation in order to inflict injury upon another? Why, or why not?
— Do you actually believe that the evil people do is returned upon them?
— Please elaborate upon your response to the divine warrior's appearance (see 3:16).
- At the end of ten minutes, invite all participants to reflect upon the questions and answers they have heard.

Dimension 3: What Does the Bible Mean to Us?

(H) Paraphrase Zephaniah 3:1-5.

- Provide class members with paper and pencils or pens.
- Remind persons that putting a biblical text in their own, contemporary words helps bring its meaning for their own lives into sharper focus.
- Encourage class members to read and then to paraphrase Zephaniah 3:1-5 while remaining faithful to the ideas these verses express.
- After ten minutes, ask volunteers to read their paraphrases to the entire class. Do they feel a stronger response thinking of these judgments on a modern city—their own city or town and their own leaders? Do they have a sense of how difficult Zephaniah's words must have been to hear to those ancient rulers and leaders?

(I) Play naysayer.

- In times of distress and discontent, we may respond to claims about God with disbelief and even anger. In the Old Testament, no less than Abraham, Moses, Habakkuk, and Job dared to express frustration and anger toward God in troubling times; and they were not rebuked for doing so. Some people of faith do not feel comfortable addressing questions much less anger to God. Many of our ancestors of faith give us models of honesty with God.

- Divide class members into three or four groups. Provide each group with Bibles, paper, and pencils or pens.
- Ask each group to read Habakkuk 1:5-11 to set the stage for the address to God. Then ask the groups to write an argument against the perspective seemingly advanced by God in Habakkuk 1:5-11.
- After the groups have written their own response to God, ask them to read the prophet's response—1:12-17.
- At the end of ten minutes, invite a representative from each group to share its arguments with the class as a whole.
— How do class members feel about expressing questions and even anger to God?
— When in their own lives have they questioned God or shown anger toward God?

(J) Examine Israel's sins and our sins.

- Divide class members into two groups. Provide each group with newsprint, an easel or stand, and a marker. Have on hand, as well, Bibles and commentaries on the books of Zephaniah and Habakkuk.
- Ask each group to select a "scribe" who will record their responses to the text.
- Suggest that **Group One** study Zephaniah 1:12-13.
— What are Israel's sins according to this passage?
- Suggest that **Group Two** study one or two of Habakkuk's "alas" oracles (2:6-20).
— What are Babylonia's sins according to the oracles they have chosen?
- After identifying Israel's and Babylonia's offenses against God, consider whether we as a society share them.
— Do we, like thieves, avail ourselves of what belongs to others?
— Do we fail to consider God's responses to our daily activities, or do we presume that the Lord is oblivious to our deeds?
- At the end of fifteen minutes, invite each group to share several of its thoughts with the class as a whole.

(K) Close by singing a hymn.

The books of Zephaniah and Habakkuk contain negative words against the nations of ancient Israel's world. The hope given in these prophetic works is that the restoration of Zion will finally bring peace and justice.

- Join in singing the hymn "For the Healing of the Nations" (*The United Methodist Hymnal*, 428), which calls for international relations characterized by justice, equality, love, and hope.

Additional Bible Helps

The Nations as God's Instruments

Frequently within ancient Israel's prophetic literature, we encounter claims that God is using foreign nations and their leaders as instruments against Israel and other peoples. Recall Habakkuk 1:5-7, with its claim that Yahweh is rousing the Chaldeans. In Isaiah 10:5-6, we read words attributed to Yahweh concerning the Assyrians:

"Ah, Assyria, the rod of my anger—
    the club in their hands is my fury!
Against a godless nation I send him,
    and against the people of my wrath I command him,
to take spoil and seize plunder,
    and to tread them down like the mire of the streets."

Jeremiah 51:7 says of Babylon:

"Babylon was a golden cup in the LORD's hand,
    making all the earth drunken;
the nations drank of her wine,
    and so the nations went mad."

Several verses later, we read the assertion that Yahweh has "stirred up the spirit of the kings of the Medes" in order to destroy Babylon (Jeremiah 51:11-12). Deutero-Isaiah insists that Yahweh strides alongside the king of Persia, Cyrus (called "[God's] anointed"), assisting him in subduing the nations (Isaiah 44:28–45:1-3).

As ancient Israel's history amply illustrates, both its Northern and Southern Kingdoms fell victim to the empire-building ambitions of the great powers of their day—the Egyptians, the Assyrians, the Babylonians, the Persians. Given Yahwistic religion's assertion that Israel's God was all-powerful, creator and sovereign of the earth and everything in it, we should not be surprised that the biblical authors nowhere ascribed Israel's military defeats to the superior force of their enemies' deities. Rather, they construed their nations' calamities as the consequences of sins committed against Yahweh. The Assyrians might destroy the city of Samaria in 721 B.C., but in fact, they were only the means by which God inflicted thoroughly merited punishment upon Israel.

This perspective had its benefits: it upheld Yahweh's supreme position among the deities of other nations and claimed history for God, rather than surrendering God to history. But it had its liabilities as well, for questions inevitably arose in its wake. One such question appears in Habakkuk 1:13b:

"Why do you look on the treacherous,
    and are silent when the wicked swallow
    those more righteous than they?"

True, Israel had sinned. But were its sins greater than those of other nations? Should not these nations, also, be held accountable by Yahweh?

The biblical prophets repeatedly insist that Yahweh's instruments of destruction will indeed be held accountable. Having described Assyria as "the rod of my anger" (Isaiah 10:5), the Isaiah tradition goes on to assert that its king shall be punished for his "arrogant boasting" and "haughty pride" (Isaiah 10:12). Assyria's king has mistakenly ascribed his military success to his own power, and he must pay for his haughtiness. After all:

> "Shall the ax vaunt itself over the one who wields it,
>   or the saw magnify itself against the one who handles it?
> As if a rod should raise the one who lifts it up,
>   or as if a staff should lift the one who is not wood!"
>
> (Isaiah 10:15)

Hence, biblical tradition responds to Habakkuk's question in 1:13b, in part, by insisting that once God's use of punitive empires has ended, they will themselves stand under Yahweh's judgment.

In this short essay, I have offered some observations concerning how ancient Israel spoke of its enemies' success in destroying its two kingdoms. In the end, however, I must conclude that such texts are problematic at a number of points. Here are four crucial questions that must be raised:

- First, what are the implications of affirming that God uses some nations as instruments of divine wrath against other nations?
- Second, what are the implications of asserting that God punishes peoples by inflicting military atrocities upon them?
- Third, what of the claim that Yahweh destroys national "instruments" once their usefulness has passed?
- Finally, what may befall a people who ascribe national disasters to the outworking of God's wrath against them?

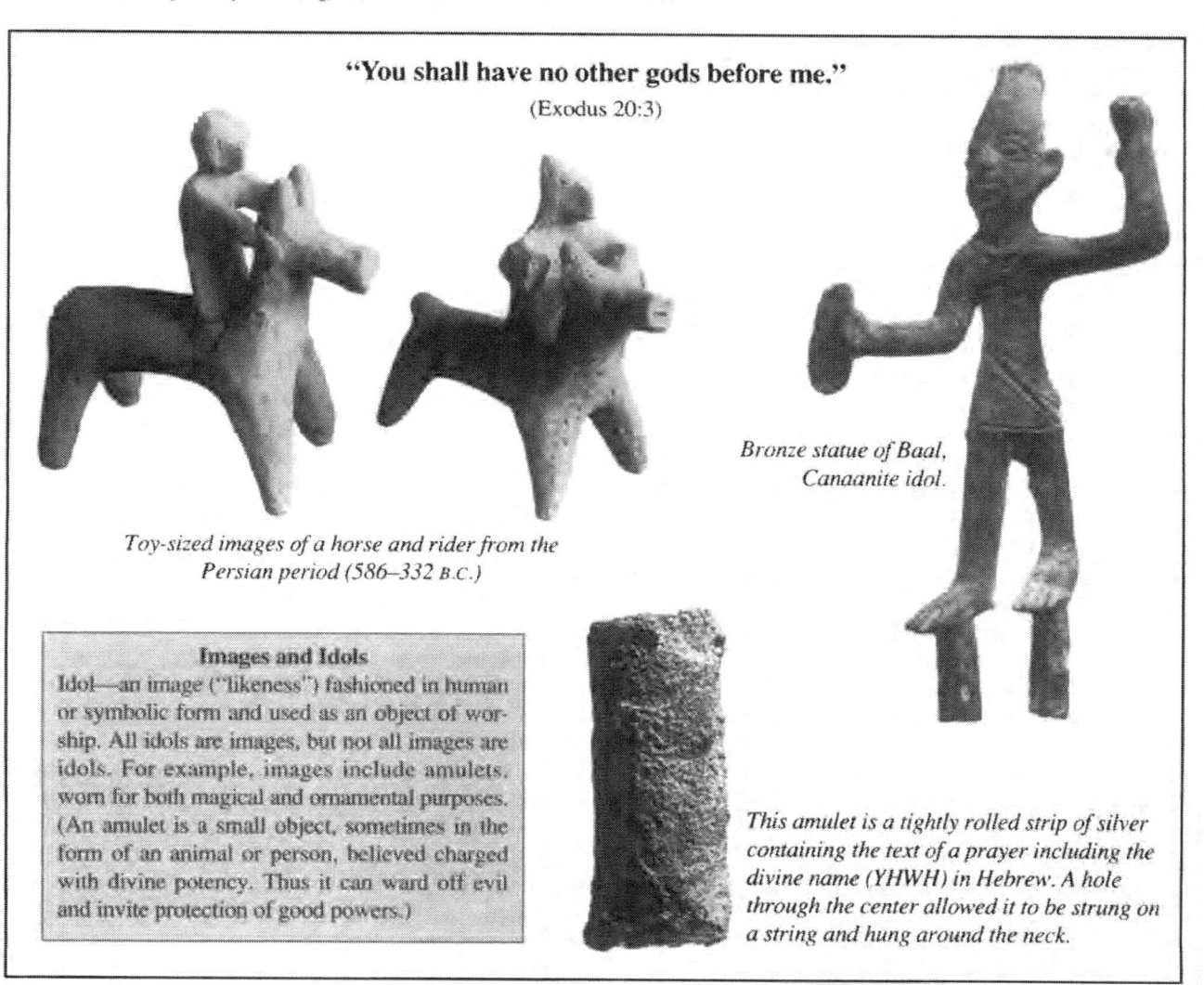

"You shall have no other gods before me."
(Exodus 20:3)

Toy-sized images of a horse and rider from the Persian period (586–332 B.C.)

Bronze statue of Baal, Canaanite idol.

Images and Idols
Idol—an image ("likeness") fashioned in human or symbolic form and used as an object of worship. All idols are images, but not all images are idols. For example, images include amulets, worn for both magical and ornamental purposes. (An amulet is a small object, sometimes in the form of an animal or person, believed charged with divine potency. Thus it can ward off evil and invite protection of good powers.)

This amulet is a tightly rolled strip of silver containing the text of a prayer including the divine name (YHWH) in Hebrew. A hole through the center allowed it to be strung on a string and hung around the neck.

10 "A Jealous and Avenging God Is the Lord"

Obadiah; Nahum

LEARNING MENU

As you study this chapter in this leader's guide, select from each of the three Dimensions those activities that you think will best serve the interests and learning styles of your class members. Spend approximately one-third of your class time working on one or two Dimension 1 activities. Two-thirds of the session, however, should be devoted to activities in Dimensions 2 and 3.

Dimension 1: What Does the Bible Say?

(A) Begin with a prayer.

A suggested opening prayer is "For Our Country," *The United Methodist Hymnal*, 429. This prayer requests God's protection, wisdom, and guidance. Note that the author is Toyohiko Kagawa. Kagawa was born in Kobe, Japan, in 1888. A Japanese social reformer, pacifist, and evangelist, he was disinherited at age fifteen for converting to Christianity. He was influential in the women's suffrage and peace movements. This prayer was first included in the author's book, *Meditations*, in 1950. Kagawa articulated pacifism in the 1930's and 1940's, which ran counter to his country's militaristic mindset (from *Companion to The United Methodist Hymnal*, by Carlton R. Young; The United Methodist Publishing House, 1993; pages 340, 779).

- You will need enough copies of *The United Methodist Hymnal* for class members to share. Read this prayer aloud together. Then share information about the author.

(B) Answer the questions in the study book.

- Discussion questions might evoke the following responses:

Nahum

1. The poet uses both literal and figurative language in describing the assault against Nineveh. We see the red shields and uniforms of the soldiers, the flash of metal fittings on the chariots. Chariots pulled by spirited horses race through the streets "like torches" and the invaders rush into the city so eagerly that they stumble.

2. The nations witnessing the shaming (destruction) of Nineveh will shrink back in disgust. But none will comfort her, since they have experienced her treachery and violence.

Obadiah

1. Obadiah 1:12-14 accuses Edom of eight offenses against Judah, its brother: gloating over Jacob's misfortune; rejoicing on the day of Judah's ruin; boasting "on the day

of distress"; entering "the gate of my people" on the day of calamity; joining in gloating over the disaster; looting Judah's goods; cutting off Judean fugitives seeking to escape; and turning them over to the Babylonian army.
2. On the Lord's day, the surviving remnant of the house of Jacob shall destroy the house of Edom and control its land.

Dimension 2: What Does the Bible Mean?

(C) Look at Nahum's opening poem.

Nahum's oracles concerning Nineveh's fall are introduced by a poem in praise of Yahweh's vengeance upon the guilty (1:2-14).

- Divide class members into three small groups. Each group will need Bibles, paper, and pens or pencils. Also you will need a chalkboard or large sheets of newsprint, chalk or markers. Write on the paper or board the characteristics and themes that each group should be looking for in the poem.
- Ask each small group to look carefully at the opening poem. Summarize the contents of the poem. Many significant themes run through the opening poem in Nahum 1:2-14. Look for the following parts and characteristics:
— the theme of vengeance (mentioned three times) and wrath against adversaries;
— attributes of God (Verse 3a affirms that God is "slow to anger," an attribute cited in other passages as well [also Nehemiah 9:17; Psalms 103:8; 145:8; Joel 2:13; Jonah 2:4]. However Nahum insists that "the LORD will by no means clear the guilty.");
— theophanic imagery (God's power [verse 3] is vividly illustrated by the theophanic imagery that follows in verses 3b-5.);
— two rhetorical questions (In verse 6 "no one" of course is the answer.).

(D) Report on some oracles.

PROPHETIC ORACLES AGAINST FOREIGN NATIONS

Oracles against foreign nations and rulers are not confined to the books of Nahum and Obadiah. To the contrary, such oracles appear in many prophetic collections.

These oracles were not actually intended for the ears of Israel's enemies. Rather, they spoke to the people of Israel and Judah.

Oracles against Israel's enemies were construed as good news for Israel, unless, of course, Israel had joined with a former adversary in an attempt to hold at bay a common foe.

- For this learning option you will need to equip three work stations with: Bibles, one-volume commentaries, paper, and pencils or pens.
- Divide class members into three groups and assign each group to a work station.
- Make the following research assignments:
— **Group One** read the following oracles: Isaiah 13 (against Babylon); Ezekiel 29:1-7 (against Egypt).
— **Group Two** read Isaiah 10:12-19 (against Assyria); Jeremiah 49:7-11 (against Edom).
— **Group Three** focus on Jeremiah 50:11-16 (against Babylon); Ezekiel 28:1-10 (against the king of Tyre).
- At the end of ten minutes, ask each group to share its passages and thoughts on those passages with the class as a whole.
- Then, as a whole class, discuss these questions:
— How are we to make sense of these passages?
— What role or roles does Yahweh play in them?
— What is the impact of claims that God fights against nations on behalf of other nations and peoples?
— How are these oracles similar to or different from the oracles found in the books of Nahum and Obadiah?

(E) Review Jacob and Esau's story.

- Before using this learning option, as the class leader you need to review the story told in Genesis about Esau and Jacob: Genesis 25:19–27:45.

TEACHING TIP

When reviewing a biblical event remember that your class members have different knowledge of the Bible and that some people remember better than others. You may want to give them time to read over the story in Genesis before you begin the oral "review," especially if you are not certain that they remember the story. If you feel comfortable that the class members know the story, you might want to play "hot potato review." Begin telling the story; then toss a "potato" (ball, or other object) to a class member. Whoever catches the "potato" must add to the story. Then the "potato" is tossed to another class member for her or his addition to the story.

Part One:
- Begin your class discussion in this manner: "We have learned in our Bible studies the important role that oral tradition held for the ancient Israelites. This was the only way to keep the story alive in those early centuries. Today we are going to try our hand at oral tradition as a form of review. In the Book of Obadiah (9-10) what ancient tradition about an Israelite patriarch is invoked by the author?" (The story of Esau and Jacob)

"Let's review that story. There was once a very faithful man named Abraham. He was married to Sarah. In their old age they had a child. The child was named Isaac. At the age of forty Isaac married Rebekah."

- Ask class members to continue the story. Listen carefully as they continue the story, adding important facts if they are omitted. (According to Genesis 25:19–27:45, the two sons of Isaac and Rebekah were at odds with each other from birth [Genesis 25:25-26]. Remember the story of how Rebekah and Jacob deceived Isaac, so that the blessing due Esau as firstborn was instead given to Jacob? Genesis 32:3–33:17 tells of an eventual reconciliation between the two brothers.)
- After class members and you have told the story of Jacob and Esau, say, "As we shall see, biblical tradition identified the Edomites as descendants of Esau, Jacob's fraternal twin. During the period of Israel's United Monarchy (that is, the reigns of David and Solomon), Israel controlled Edomite territory (strategic because of its trade routes). In subsequent centuries, however, Judah and Edom often fought for control of the land." (See, for example, 2 Kings 14:22; 16:6.)
- After reviewing the story of Esau and Jacob read aloud Obadiah 10-14.

Part Two:
- After you have reviewed the story of Esau and Jacob and have seen its role in the Book of Obadiah, try your hand at rewriting how Edom could have treated his brother.
- Divide class members into three or four small groups. Supply each group with paper and pens or pencils.
- Tell each group to reread verses 10-14 thinking how Edom might have treated Judah (Jacob).
- Ask a representative from each group to report on their group's ideas to the whole class.

(F) Ask questions of Obadiah.

- Prior to class time write the four questions posed in this learning option on the chalkboard or on large sheets of newsprint so that everyone can see them.
- Divide class members into conversation groups of two or three persons. Ask them, in light of their reading of Obadiah, to consider the following questions:
—What does this book tell us about God?
—What does it tell us about human nature?
—What does it tell us about our relationship with God?
—What does it tell us about our relationships with, and responsibilities to, persons in and beyond our own communities?
- At the end of ten minutes, ask one person from each group to report to the class a summary of that group's responses to one of the four questions posed.

(G) Research the Assyrian Empire and the nation of Edom.

- For this option you will need research stations equipped with Bibles, Bible dictionaries, paper, and pencils.

- Divide class members into four groups. Assign each group to a research station.
—**Groups One** and **Two** will research the Assyrian Empire. Each group should take notes on information that seems especially pertinent to this lesson.
—**Groups Three** and **Four** will research the nation of Edom. Again, each group should take notes on information that seems especially pertinent to this lesson.
- At the end of fifteen minutes, ask representatives from each group to share its findings with the class as a whole.

(H) Write from the Assyrians' perspective.

- In this learning option your class members will have the opportunity to write, from the Assyrians' perspective, an account of the destruction of their capital city, Nineveh.
- Class members will need paper and pencils or pens.
- Ask them to compose a newspaper article on the breaking story of Nineveh's overthrow. They may wish to work in groups, in pairs, or individually.
- Remind them of the who, what, where, when, and why of journalism. Encourage them to make use of "anonymous sources" and "government insiders."
- Persons may wish to include in their articles a quotation from a priest of the god Asshur's cult. How could an Assyrian deity permit the Ninevites to suffer so?
- At the end of ten minutes, invite class members/groups to share their articles with the entire class.

Dimension 3:
What Does the Bible Mean to Us?

(I) Evaluate a recent catastrophe.

- For this learning option you will need large sheets of newsprint, tape, and markers or chalkboard and chalk. Also you will need a current newspaper or some news magazines.
- Recruit one class member to act as "scribe" for the group.
- Drawing from national news reports and newspaper headlines, select a story concerning national or international strife.
- Ask participants to discuss the following questions:
—How, given his cultural presuppositions and theological premises, might Nahum (or Obadiah) have spoken concerning such a calamity?
—How might he describe God's relationship to human suffering in that particular situation?
—In what ways might our understandings and approaches to the crisis differ from these prophets', given our own presuppositions and theological beliefs?

—In what ways do we, as Christians, understand God's relationship to persons and nations undergoing such catastrophes?

(J) Invite your pastor to this session.

> Prior to class time talk with your pastor and invite him or her to visit your class session. Ask if she or he would be willing to talk with your class members about the oracles against foreign nations found in Nahum and Obadiah. Have on hand a copy of the following questions, which might serve as starting points for your pastor's remarks.

- In preparation to using this learning option, read the article "Oracles Against Foreign Nations and Rulers" found in the "Additional Bible Helps" on page 52.
- Welcome your pastor and help facilitate the discussion of the following questions:
—How do we, as Christians, both understand these oracles within their original cultural and social contexts and search out their meaning for today?
—Have such oracles a place in our faith communities' prayers and conversations about contemporary battles between nations and peoples? If so, how?
—Have we the freedom to enter into dialogues with these biblical books, realizing that such dialogues may place us at odds with them?
—Do other passages within our Hebrew Scriptures articulate additional ways of understanding Israel's relations with the nations? (Refer to Genesis 12:2-3.)
—When have you chosen to use Scripture passages from these prophetic books to inform and direct your sermon and the worship service?

(K) Compose a communal lament.

- In this learning option you will be asking class members to compose a communal lament on behalf of a people or nation suffering violence from its neighbors.
- For this activity you will need large sheets of newsprint or posterboard, tape, markers, and newspapers or news magazines.
- Every day's news brings word of tragic battles somewhere in our world.
- Divide class members into three or four groups.
- Each group should have newsprint and markers.
- Ask each group to identify a particular crisis, at home or abroad, the group wishes to lament in prayer to God. Have current newspapers available in case one of the groups needs help getting started.
- Each group should then compose a lament—an expression of sorrow, of concern for those who suffer, of frustration, and even of anger over that crisis.

- Groups may reflect upon God's role in the midst of suffering in ways that differ from Nahum and Obadiah's ways. And, of course, their laments may well reflect the centrality of Christ for Christian faith.
- At the end of ten minutes, ask each group to display its lament before the class as a whole.
- Taking turns, each group should lead the class in praying its lament.
- You may want to make smaller copies of these laments and offer them to your pastor to incorporate into a Sunday worship service during the prayer time.

(L) Learn about vengeance and reconciliation.

- In this learning option you will be exploring the idea of choosing vengeance or reconciliation.

> If you have an attorney in your class or congregation invite him or her ahead of time to join your class session for a discussion of our legal system. Tell him or her that you will be discussing our legal system from the biblical points of view of vengeance and reconciliation. A balanced discussion would be to invite both a defense and a prosecuting attorney. In inviting individuals to represent these two views, try to invite people who are friends. Be sure that this does not feel like you are "setting them up" for a negative experience, only to share their ideas.

- To begin this discussion summarize the information given in the "Additional Bible Helps" that addresses the prophetic oracles that call for vengeance from God. Also read on page 83 in the study book in Dimension 3 about cries for vengeance becoming acts of vengeance.
- Next ask three class members to read the following New Testament passages:
—Matthew 18:15-20 (on reproving one's brother)
—Matthew 18:21-22 (on reconciliation)
—Luke 17:4 (on reconciliation)
- The stage is now set for discussion. In the Bible we hear cries for vengeance and strong words of forgiveness. How do we, a people of faith, deal with injustices?
—When we have fallen victim to a crime what are our cries? (If someone has been a victim and feels comfortable ask her or him to share from personal experience her or his feelings.)
—Does our legal system lean more to the side of reconciliation or vengeance? Why do you think that is so?
—How is reconciliation addressed?
—If you have attorneys present, ask them when have they experienced people requesting reconciliation.

(M) Close with a hymn.

- For this closing hymn you will need copies of *The United Methodist Hymnal*. Try to recruit a pianist to accompany

class members. The suggested closing hymn for today's lesson is "This Is My Song" (No. 437). This hymn is sung to a familiar hymn tune—also used with "Be Still, My Soul," No. 534— in case an accompanist is not available.
- You may want to point out these relationships between the hymn and the biblical books studied today:
—Both the biblical books and the hymn have a strong nationalistic theme;
—Both desire God as the "God of all the nations";
—However, the hymn also recognizes the integrity of other nations.

Additional Bible Helps

Oracles Against Foreign Nations and Rulers
With the exception of Hosea, all the prophetic books in our Hebrew Scriptures contain oracles against foreign nations. Despite their numbers, however, such oracles are seldom the focus of sermons, Bible studies, and religious education studies. Their neglect is, in many ways, understandable. As the books of Nahum and Obadiah illustrate, such oracles often are characterized by cries for vengeance and grisly scenes of suffering and destruction. What place have they among faith communities—Jewish and Christian—whose prayers and hymns would focus, instead, upon hopes for peace and understanding among nations?

In the world of ancient Israel, curses against foreign nations often were part of preparations for warfare. In Numbers 22–24, for example, we read how Balak (BAY-lak), the king of Moab, attempted to hired Balaam (BAY-luhm), the diviner, to pronounce a curse over the Israelites as they camped in the plains of Moab, seemingly posing a threat to his kingdom. According to this tradition, Balaam was constrained from cursing Israel by Yahweh, who commanded that he bless the people instead. The story suggests, nonetheless, that bringing a divine curse against one's enemies was believed to facilitate victory.

Both 1 Samuel 15:2-3 and 1 Kings 20:26-30 tell of incidents in which prophetic figures indicted Israel's enemies for particular offenses and then spurred the Israelites to battle on the basis of those offenses. In both cases, of course, the prophets' words were spoken to Israelites, rather than to the enemies themselves. We can reasonably construe that one of the purposes of such oracles was to convince Israel's forces that God supported their cause and would insure victory.

Although biblical oracles against foreign nations and rulers address those parties directly, the prophets were not actually speaking to the Egyptians, Assyrians, Babylonians, and so on. Their words, too, were intended for the ears of their Israelite audiences. What were some of the functions of these oracles?

- First, these oracles affirmed the universal sovereignty of Israel's God. Other nations might place trust in their respective gods and goddesses, but the prophets' words of judgment and destruction were proclaimed in Yahweh's name. If Yahweh were capable of punishing the great empires of the ancient world, then no deity could rival the power of Israel's God.

- Second, oracles against foreign nations and rulers reminded Israel that God's judgment extended to other nations, as well as to itself. The prophet Habakkuk undoubtedly was not alone when he questioned the justice of wicked nations defeating peoples more righteous than they (1:13). These oracles asserted, however, that Yahweh held Israel's enemies accountable for their pride, greed, violence, and oppression.

- Third, such oracles, especially in their canonical contexts, functioned as preludes to Israel's salvation and restoration. The downfall of a hostile nation was in itself potentially good news for its victims. In several prophetic collections, however, oracles against foreign nations are sandwiched between judgment oracles against Israel and promises of redemption for its future, functioning as a sort of pivot between the two.

For learning option (I) in the next lesson you will need a photocopy of the article on pages 71 and 72, "Watching in the Night Visions: Daniel's Apocalypse and Early Christian Reflection on Jesus," for every class member.

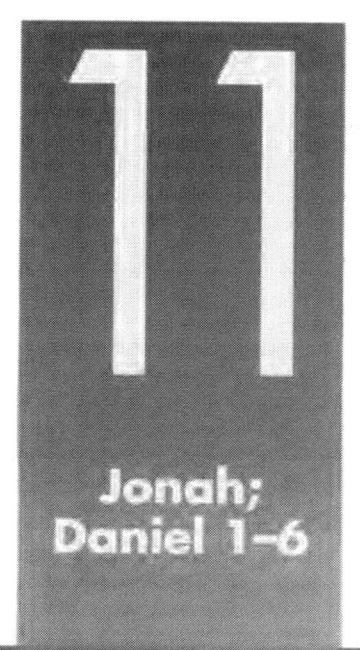

11
"I Called to the Lord Out of My Distress and He Answered Me"

Jonah; Daniel 1–6

LEARNING MENU

Keeping in mind the ways in which your class members learn best, as well as their needs and interests, choose at least one learning option from each of the three Dimensions.

Dimension 1: What Does the Bible Say?

(A) Join in a "Canticle of Light and Darkness."

The following "Canticle of Light and Darkness" appears in *The United Methodist Hymnal*, No. 205.

- Ask class members to join in singing (if hymnals are available) or saying the words of the following response:

  "You are the light of the world;
   be light in our darkness, O Christ."

- Ask three persons to lead the group in praying the passages of the Canticle (Isaiah 9:2; 59:9-10; Psalm 139:11-12; Daniel 2:20, 22; 1 John 1:5).

(B) Answer the questions in the study book.

- Discussion of Dimension 1 questions might include the following responses:

Jonah
1. Jonah books passage on a ship bound for Tarshish—that is, instead of heading east, he heads west, apparently on the premise that he can escape God and God's command.
2. All the inhabitants of Nineveh, from king to cattle, observe a fast and don sackcloth. Moreover, the king issues a proclamation requiring that in addition to these rituals, all should "cry mightily to God. All shall turn from their evil ways and from the violence that is in their hands. Who knows? God may relent and change his mind; he may turn from his fierce anger, so that we do not perish" (3:8-9).

   Jonah first responds by seeking to justify his earlier decision to escape Yahweh's command: "That is why I fled to Tarshish at the beginning; for I knew that you are a gracious God and merciful, slow to anger, and abounding in steadfast love, and ready to relent from punishing." God's reputation for unmerited mercy angers Jonah in this context. Having made this point, Jonah goes outside the city to see what its fate shall be. God, in turn, challenges Jonah's self-absorption and lack of compassion for Nineveh's inhabitants.

Daniel

1. At the end of ten days, Daniel and his friends appear healthier and better nourished than the other men in Nebuchadnezzar's training program. God rewards these devout Jews who maintain Jewish dietary laws, even when the rich delicacies and wine of the king's own table are available to them. At the end of the three-year training period, Nebuchadnezzar concludes that Daniel and his friends are ten times better in "every matter of wisdom and understanding" than all of the magicians and enchanters in his entire kingdom. He therefore stations them within his own court (1:19-21), where Daniel remains for some seventy years.

Additional Information: During Daniel's involvement in the courts of the kings, tradition has it that Daniel served for over seventy years. Four different kings are mentioned in the Book of Daniel under whom Daniel served: Nebuchadnezzar (2:1), Belshazzar (5:1), Darius the Mede (5:30), and Cyrus (6:28). Some of the historical references in Daniel are correct, while others do not line up with secular records. If your class members are interested in more information about the various kings whom Daniel served under, consult a commentary introduction to Daniel or a Bible dictionary such as *Harper's Bible Dictionary*.

2. Nebuchadnezzar falls on his face and worships Daniel, commanding that a grain offering and incense be offered to him (as if he were a god!). But he also praises Daniel's God as "God of gods and Lord of kings and a revealer of mysteries" (2:47). Daniel receives a promotion, as well as "many great gifts"; at his request, Shadrach, Meshach, and Abednego also receive promotions placing them over "the affairs of the province of Babylon."

Dimension 2: What Does the Bible Mean?

(C) Question Jonah and Daniel.

- Ahead of time write the four questions on the chalkboard or on large sheets of newsprint or posterboard. These general questions of the Book of Jonah and of the Book of Daniel will serve as excellent starting points for your study.
- Divide class members into two conversation groups.
- Ask **Group One** to work with the Book of Jonah. Ask them, in light of their reading of Jonah 1, to consider the questions below and in the next column:
- Ask **Group Two** to work with the Book of Daniel. Ask them also, in light of their reading of Daniel 1–2, to consider the following questions.
—What does this passage tell us about God?
—What does it tell us about human nature?
—What does it tell us about our relationship with God?
—What does it tell us about our relationships with, and responsibilities to, others?
- At the end of ten minutes, ask one person from each group to share with the class a summary of that group's responses to one of the four questions.

(D) Create a picture poem.

- For this learning option you will need paper, large sheets of newsprint or posterboard, and markers.

> The final suggested activity for this option is to work on a picture poem. A picture poem uses words or phrases to outline the shape of an object. The story will be told very briefly for this kind of poem. It is best if the picture or shape symbolizes the story.

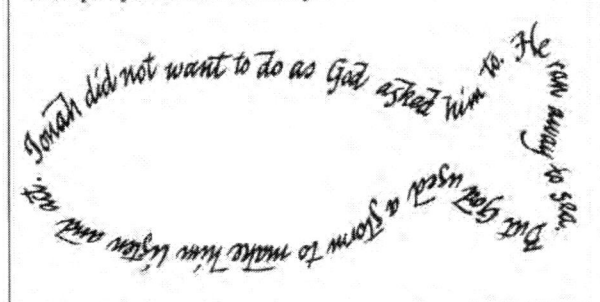

Art and picture poem suggestion from *New Ways to Tell the Old, Old Story*, by Delia Halverson. Copyright © 1992 by Abingdon Press. Used by permission.

- Divide class members into two groups. Group One will be working with the Book of Jonah and Group Two will be working with the Book of Daniel. Explain to them what is meant by a picture poem. Ensure that both groups have a copy of the questions for their study.

Group One:
Read Jonah 1:4–2:10. Answer the following questions:
—How does Jonah respond to the sailors' question concerning what must be done in order for the storm to subside (1:11-16)?
—What do the sailors do? (Jonah informs the terrified sailors that they must throw him into the sea, "for I know it is because of me that this great storm has come upon you" [1:12]. Despite Jonah's words, the sailors continue to battle the storm, until it becomes so severe that they have no choice but to throw Jonah overboard. Nevertheless, they do so with a prayer to Yahweh on their lips that they not be held accountable for the loss of Jonah's life.)
—What is the outcome?
—How did Jonah survive?
- Work together as a group and draw a picture poem to tell your story.

Group Two:
Read Daniel 6. Then answer the following questions:

—Why was there a plot against Daniel?
—Did the king support the prayer law?
—What is Daniel's punishment?
—What is the outcome?
—Does the prayer appearing in Daniel 6:26-27 provide a clue to an important function of the story of Daniel in the lions' den? (By placing words of praise to God in the mouth of Darius, king of "all peoples and nations of every language throughout the whole world," the biblical author asserts in a most powerful way the unrivaled sovereignty and power of Israel's God.)
- Work together as a group and draw a picture poem to tell your story.
- After about ten minutes, ask a representative from each group to show its picture poem and tell the story.

(E) Join Jonah on a tour of the city of Nineveh.

- Ask one member of the class to assume the role of Jonah as he travels one day's distance into the city of Nineveh. Ask another person to play the role of a descendant of an Israelite family that took up residence in Nineveh following the destruction of the Northern Kingdom of Israel and the deportation of its inhabitants. Ask four or five other class members to play the roles of curious Ninevites.
- Provide space at the front of the classroom for the tour to take place. Allow your volunteers several minutes to "get into character."
- As Jonah and his companion walk through the streets of Nineveh, Jonah should offer characteristic comments about its sinfulness and the justice of God's decision to destroy the city. The companion may have a different perspective, having lived among the city's inhabitants and come to know some of them as persons and not just as the "other."
- Jonah and his companion may pause from time to time to speak with Ninevites they encounter along the way.
- At the end of ten to fifteen minutes, allow time for class members to discuss what they have seen and heard. At what points do they agree or disagree with the actors?

(F) Write an epilogue.

- The Book of Jonah ends with Yahweh's speech to the sulking prophet.
- Give each class member paper and a pencil. You will need to have extra Bibles on hand.
- Recruit a class member to read aloud Jonah 4.
- Then ask everyone to compose an epilogue (final speech) by Jonah in response to God's remarks and final question.
- Some class members may compose a speech in which Jonah himself repents of his previous attitudes. Others may imagine that Jonah persists in his anger.
- At the end of ten minutes, ask for volunteers to read their speeches to the class as a whole.

(G) Picture Daniel's dream vision.

Daniel's dream vision in chapter 7 describes the fates of mighty world empires and the coming of God's kingdom. Its symbolism is best understood with the assistance of Bible commentaries.

- For this learning option you will need to equip three research stations with Bibles, Bible commentaries on the Book of Daniel, paper, and pencils or pens. Also if you want to do **Part Two** of this option you will need paper, pencils, crayons, markers, glitter, glue, construction paper, and other art materials.
- Divide class members into three groups, and assign each group to a research station. Assign the following verses to each group:
—Group One—7:1-8
—Group Two—7:9-18
—Group Three—7:19-28

Part One:
- Tell each group to search for the hidden meanings of the symbolism and to try to find out which world empires are described.
- At the end of fifteen minutes, ask a representative of each group to share its findings with the entire class.

Part Two:
- These three Scripture passages are rich with images. Keeping the same Scripture passage, ask each small group to draw pictures of these images.
- After each group has had a chance do a picture, have a representative tell about the vision.
- After each group has made its presentation, Ask the class as a whole to reflect on the message of this apocalyptic (pertaining to a prophetic disclosure) chapter.

(H) Investigate Daniel's prayer and Gabriel's response.

In the opening verses of chapter 9, Daniel investigates the meaning of Jeremiah's prophecies concerning the seventy years of Israel's exile (Jeremiah 25:11-12; 29:10).

Daniel's prayer in 9:4-19 confesses Israel's history of sinfulness and its consequences.

At the conclusion of that prayer, Gabriel addresses Daniel and explains the significance of Jeremiah's words, as well as how future events shall unfold.

- Reading the section, "Revelation as Interpretation" in the "Additional Bible Helps" (page 57), will give you background information for leading the discussion for this option.
- For this learning option you will need three research stations equipped with Bibles, Bible commentaries on the Book of Daniel, paper, and pencils or pens.
- Divide class members into three groups and assign each

group to a research station. Share the above information on Daniel 9 with your class members as a form of introduction to this learning option. Ask the small groups to research these following passages and to bring their findings back to the whole class. Assign the following verses to each group:
—**Group One**—9:1-10
—**Group Two**—9:11-19
—**Group Three**—9:20-27
- At the end of fifteen minutes, invite a representative of each group to share its findings with the entire class.
- After each group has made its presentation, invite the class as a whole to reflect on the message of this apocalyptic chapter.

Dimension 3:
What Does the Bible Mean to Us?

(I) Learn about Daniel's Apocalypse and Jesus.

In this learning option you will be discussing "Watching in the Night Visions: Daniel's Apocalypse and Early Christian Reflection on Jesus," page 71 in this leader's guide.
- Make a copy of this article for every member of the class.

DEFINITIONS
Apocalyptic (uh-pok-uh-LIP-tik)—pertaining to a prophetic disclosure or revelation. (See more in the "Glossary," study book, page 112.)
Revelation—a dramatic disclosure of something not previously known. A manifestation of divine will.
Eschatology (es-kuh-TOL-uh-jee)—teaching concerning the end of history.

- Write the following questions on a chalkboard or on large sheets of newsprint taped on the wall, so that class members can read the questions.
- Divide class members into small groups to discuss questions. Allow five to ten minutes for them to read the article. Then ask them to discuss the article in light of the questions on the board.
- After several minutes, ask volunteers from each group to respond to some or all of the following questions:
—Were you previously aware of the role of apocalyptic in early Christian theology?
—What are the advantages and dangers of apocalyptic thinking?
—Why were Jewish and early Christian apocalyptic groups especially attracted to the oracles of earlier prophetic advocates of the poor and downtrodden?
—What were the effects of Greek culture upon the Jews and Jewish apocalyptic?
—Why did Jewish apocalyptic wane in the years following the destruction of the second Temple in A.D. 70?
—What aspects of early Christianity became more important as the influence of apocalyptic decreased?
—To what do future "son of man" passages in the Gospels refer? What ideas are associated with present "son of man" passages?

(J) Pray with Jonah and Daniel.

In this learning option you will be joining with characters in Jonah and Daniel in prayers of thanksgiving and praise to God.
- If possible, arrange the chairs in your classroom into a circle.
- Recruit three Scripture readers.
—**Reader One**—Jonah 2:2
—**Reader Two**—Daniel 2:20-22
—**Reader Three**—Daniel 4:34b-35, 37b
- Ask participants to pray silently about some aspect of Jonah's message that speaks to a personal need for spiritual growth and action in their own lives.
- After several minutes, ask Reader One to read aloud Jonah 2:2.
- Then ask class members to pray silently about a time when they have trusted in God, despite uncertainty and fear.
- After several minutes, ask Reader Two to read aloud Daniel 2:20-22.
- Now allow class members several minutes to offer a silent prayer of consecration to God's will for their lives.
- When they have finished, ask Reader Three to read aloud Daniel 4:34b-35, 37b. End with "Amen."

(K) Identify shortcomings.

- Divide class members into two groups. Provide each group with newsprint, an easel or stand or tape, and a marker. Have on hand, as well, Bibles and commentaries on the books of Jonah and Daniel.
- Ask each group to select a "scribe" who will use marker and newsprint to record the group's responses to the text.
- **Group One** will study Jonah 4.
—What are Jonah's shortcomings according to this passage?
- **Group Two** will study Daniel 9:4-14.
—What have been Israel's shortcomings according to Daniel's prayer?
- After identifying Jonah's and Israel's offenses against God, consider whether we as a society share them.
—Do we, like Jonah, wish to reserve God's mercy for ourselves, excluding those we dismiss as "the least of these"?
—Do we fail to consider God's responses to our daily activities, presuming that the Lord is either oblivious or not interested in our deeds?
- At the end of fifteen minutes, invite each group to share several of its thoughts with the class as a whole.

(L) Close with a meditation.

(This closing meditation is adapted and reprinted by permission from *Places Along the Way: Meditations on the Journey of Faith*, by Martin Marty, copyright © 1994 Augsburg Fortress.)

- Ask class members to sit comfortably and to listen to this closing reading. Try to have a large picture of a great bustling city, like Tokyo, Rio de Janeiro, or New York City to display. (This could be found in a newspaper, a news magazine, or a *National Geographic*.) Tape this picture on the wall so that class members can see it during the reading.

"*Nineveh*. That great city is so like the cities of our time. The mention of Nineveh calls to mind any place that is great, ungovernable, inhumane—and far from God. These cities—and towns too, for that matter—stand under judgment. So do ours.

"It would be easy to write them off, to be unconcerned about them, to let them go their own way while we carve out little corners where we can pursue spiritual safety. Before we do so, however, Nineveh [deserves] a second look.

". . . [The] metropolis was doomed, and Jonah was to be the voice of its doom. The prophet did everything he could to evade the call of God to pronounce judgment, but in the end he did preach. Then, to his almost horrified surprise, 'the people of Nineveh believed God' (3:5). They proclaimed a fast.

". . . 'God changed his mind' and spared Nineveh (3:10). This change is . . . astonishing." Jonah could not welcome this divine mercy. But God is "gracious and spares the repentant. In ancient cities and today, God spares us."

Additional Bible Helps

(The following paragraphs concerning the Book of Daniel are excerpted from Dr. John J. Collins' book, *The Apocalyptic Vision of the Book of Daniel* [Scholars Press, 1977; pages 74-76], and are used by permission. Dr. Collins serves as an Old Testament Editor for *The New Interpreter's Bible* commentary series published by Abingdon Press.)

Revelation as Interpretation

"In the tales, Daniel appears as a wise interpreter, endowed with 'knowledge and understanding of books and learning of every kind' and he has a particular gift for 'interpreting visions and dreams of every kind' (1:17). His skills are illustrated by interpretations of dreams in chs. 2 and 4 and by reading the writing on the wall in ch. 5. In chs. 7-12, Daniel is no longer the interpreter, but the recipient of revelation. However, this revelation is not communicated directly, but through the mediation of an angel who explains Daniel's visions in chs. 7 and 8, and interprets the prophecy of Jeremiah in ch. 9. Again, in ch. 11, while the angel is speaking directly to Daniel, he is only communicating to him 'what is written in the book of Truth' (10:21).

"There is an obvious similarity between the role of Daniel as interpreter of dreams and signs in chs. 2 and 5 and that of the interpreting angel in chs. 7-12. In ch. 2, Daniel's prayer is answered in a vision of the night, without reference to an angel. The angel might then appear superfluous in the second half of the book. The fact that he is introduced there serves to emphasize that revelation is a mystery in the visions of Daniel, just as it is in the dreams of Nebuchadnezzar. In neither half of the book is the word of the Lord given directly to men as it was to the classical Hebrew prophets. Instead, revelation is given first in a cryptic form, whether in dreams or visions, mysterious writing or biblical prophecy. The reception of revelation calls not for the obedience of the prophet, but for the wisdom of an interpreter, and this wisdom itself derives from a heavenly source. The function of Daniel in the tales is taken over by the angel in the visions. In both cases interpreters are necessary. The revelation is mysterious and not amenable to direct understanding.

. . . .

"We touch here on a fundamental distinction between prophecy and apocalyptic. The prophetic oracle is addressed directly to the people, calling for decision and repentance. The visions of destruction which they see could conceivably be averted. In Amos 7:4 the prophet sees a typically apocalyptic vision: 'The Lord God was calling for a judgment by fire, and it devoured the great deep and was eating up the land.' But then 'the Lord repented concerning this: "This also shall not be" saith the Lord.' Such a reprieve is no longer possible in apocalyptic, no matter how the people repent. An apocalyptic writing such as Daniel is not communicating a conditional threat. It is interpreting what has already been revealed in cryptic form. Its future predictions have the character of *information* rather than threats or promises. The mysteries contained in either visions, dreams or writings are already set. Nothing the audience can do will change the course of events. All they can do is understand and adapt to the inevitable."

12 "Everyone Who Calls on the Name of the Lord Shall Be Saved"

Joel

LEARNING MENU
Based upon your knowledge of class members, their interests and needs, and the learning approaches that prove most successful, choose at least one exercise from each of the following three Dimensions. Spend approximately one-third of class time working on one or both Dimension 1 activities. Remember, however, that approximately two-thirds of class time should be spent on options in Dimensions 2 and 3.

Dimension 1: What Does the Bible Say?

(A) Begin with a hymn to God, the Creator.

"God, Who Stretched the Spangled Heavens" (*The United Methodist Hymnal*, 150), both praises God as creator and asks for divine guidance in the use of our modern technologies.
- Invite class members to join in singing this hymn together. If you have a pianist in your class ask him or her to accompany your class members in the singing of this hymn.
- If this hymn is unfamiliar, participants can read the stanzas responsively.
- After singing or reading responsively you may want to point out the following points about the hymn:

  In stanzas two and three the author contrasts the human endeavor, imagination, and skill expended in space exploration with our seeming inability to deal with the earthly realities of lifeless, faceless, and lonely cities. Also the possibility of eliminating God's gift of creation in a nuclear holocaust is mentioned. The freedom of science comes with a responsibility to creation (from *Companion to The United Methodist Hymnal*, by Carlton R. Young; The United Methodist Publishing House, 1993; pages 374–75).

  The Book of Joel is filled with agricultural images. In these vivid images we learn more of humanity's relationship to the earth and its fruits and God's power over all.

(B) Answer the questions in the study book.

- Discussion questions might evoke the following responses:
1. Joel uses a rich array of metaphors and similes in his descriptions of the desert locust storm: they are "a nation [that has] invaded my land"; "its teeth are lions' teeth, and it has the fangs of a lioness." Joel 2:4-5 likens the locusts to a vast invading army, with war-horses and chariots, and to a raging fire that destroys everything in its path. Verse 9 describes their assault upon the city, where they "enter through the windows like a thief."

These verses (1:7, 12) provide vivid descriptions of the locusts' devastating effects upon Israel's sources of food: vines, fig trees, wheat and barley, and fruit trees.

> **TEACHING TIP**
>
> A quick review of the use of metaphor and simile:
>
> **Metaphor**—A figure of speech in which a term is transferred from the object it ordinarily designates to an object it may designate only by implicit comparison (example—its [locusts'] teeth are lions' teeth).
>
> **Simile (SIM-uh-lee)**—A figure of speech in which two essentially unlike things are compared, often in a phrase introduced by like or as (example—where they enter through the windows like a thief).

2. So cataclysmic are the effects of the locust plague that it quickens thoughts of the "day of the LORD." As noted in previous lessons, the day of the Lord was popularly conceived as a time when Yahweh would take vengeance against Israel's foes. The eighth-century prophets reversed popular expectations, proclaiming that on Yahweh's day, the Lord would punish Israel for its sins. Later, apocalyptic writers returned to the notion that the day of the Lord would mark God's battle against all sinful powers. In the first half of the Book of Joel, Israel stands under judgment and so interprets the current crisis as a manifestation, or portent of God's approaching day. Hence, it repents of its sinfulness. In the second half of the book, however, the day of the Lord is imagined as God's final victory against the nations; while "those who call on the name of the LORD" shall be saved.
3. God calls the people of Israel to genuine acts of contrition, lament, and repentance. The poet extends hope that Yahweh will relent from punishing the people and "leave a blessing behind him, a grain offering and a drink offering for the LORD, your God."
4. The description of conditions that shall appear in Israel following Yahweh's decisive victory against evil powers is Eden-like, exceeding normal conditions in nature under even the most favorable circumstances. Egypt and Edom, by contrast, will be reduced to uninhabited wasteland because of the violence they have inflicted upon God's people.

Dimension 2: What Does the Bible Mean?

(C) Communicate through poetry.

Part One:
Poetry can convey very powerful images and messages. Listen to what the prophet Joel says in his lament over the ruin of his country.

- Recruit five readers. Assign them the following verses to read aloud:
  - **Reader One**—Joel 1:2–3
  - **Reader Two**—Joel 1:4
  - **Reader Three**—Joel 1:5–7
  - **Reader Four**—Joel 1:8–10
  - **Reader Five**—Joel 1:11–12
- Our ancient Hebrew ancestors believed that God was responsible for natural disasters. The cause of the images conveyed in the first twelve verses of chapter 1 are attributed to Yahweh. How can these natural devastations be made to cease?
- Now read verse 13 in unison. (Be sure you have copies of the same translation of the Bible for everyone to use.)

Part Two:
The language of poetry can, in its own way, convey the seriousness of a present-day ecological problem as powerfully as can scientific descriptions.

- Divide class members into groups of three or four persons. Provide each group with a Bible, as well as paper and pens or pencils.
- Ask each group to identify a contemporary crisis threatening our planet and to compose several lines of verse concerning this problem.
- Encourage participants not to give up too quickly. Their efforts need not result in polished poems. The point of this exercise is to explore metaphors, similes, and other uses of language to describe a phenomenon through a different medium of expression.
- At the end of fifteen minutes, ask someone from each group to read its composition to the entire class.
- Allow several minutes for discussion after the presentations.
- If your class members have chosen to do both Part One and Part Two, then ask them the following questions:
  - What are the similarities and differences in our poems and the ancient biblical poems?
  - Do both use metaphors, similes, and other figures of speech to convey meaning and feelings in the poems?
  - The ancient people of faith believed that true repentance would right the natural disaster wrongs. How do modern-day people of faith try to correct ecological problems? How do you account for the different approaches?

(D) Paraphrase God's marvelous promises to Zion.

Part One:
In Joel 2:26-27 God promises Zion's inhabitants plenty to eat and that they will never be put to shame again.

- Read these verses aloud. Ask the following questions:
  - In verse 26 what is being promised? (Joel 2:26 promises that Israel shall again have enough to eat, causing it to praise the name of Yahweh for God's wondrous dealings with the people.)

—What promise is being made in verse 27? (According to 2:17, the temple priests entreat God to spare the people, lest they and God become a mockery among the nations. The last line of verse 26 announces that God's people "shall never again be put to shame"; this reassurance is repeated in verse 27. In the face of Yahweh's deliverance, the people of Israel will recognize that their God, who has no rivals, is in their midst.)

Part Two:
- After reflecting on Joel 2:26-27, divide class members into three or four groups. Supply each with paper and pencils.
- Ask each group to paraphrase these ancient words of assurance. Write the paraphrase from God's point of view to them—your congregation.
- After about ten minutes ask a representative to read each group's words to the whole class.

(E) Imagine the dreams and visions of those who receive God's spirit.

According to Joel 2:28-29, all God's people shall dream dreams and see visions.
- Read these verses aloud.
- Divide class members into groups identified in this passage: Israelite sons, daughters, old men, young men, male slaves, and female slaves.
- Allow several minutes for these groups to reflect on what their dreams and visions might be, given their assumed ages, genders, and social locations within Israelite society.
- Invite each person to share his or her dreams and visions with the entire class.
- Next, ask class members to identify what their own dreams and visions for the future might be.

(F) Write an account of the locust plague for your local newspaper.

- Provide participants with paper and pencils or pens.
- Ask class members to compose a newspaper article on the breaking story of a severe locust attack. They may wish to work in pairs or individually.
- Remember the who, what, where, when, and why of journalism.
- At the end of ten minutes, ask individuals or pairs to read their articles to the entire class.
- Then discuss the following questions:
—What are some of our modern-day "plagues"?
—How as a society do we address these problems?
—Do you think that these "plagues" are God-sent?

(G) Make a collage.

The tragedy endured by ancient Israel and its land becomes real to us when we depict it using pictures from trouble spots around today's world.

- Divide class members into groups of three. Give each group three to four news and agricultural magazines, posterboard, scissors, markers, and glue.
- Ask each group to make a collage that illustrates catastrophes like those described in the Book of Joel.
- At the end of fifteen minutes, invite each group to share its artwork with the class as a whole.
- Class members may wish to display their collages in the classroom.
—We know that ancient Israel's response to these disasters was to "put on sackcloth and lament" (1:13). What is our modern-day response to drought, famine, and pestilence?

Dimension 3: What Does the Bible Mean to Us?

(H) Find images to describe God.

The second half of the Book of Joel reflects ancient Israel's wish that enemy nations be destroyed by Yahweh in a final victory and that God's people be exalted.

- For this learning option you will need a chalkboard and chalk or a large sheet of paper and markers.
- Ask two class members to read aloud Joel 3:9-21: the first will read verses 9-16; the second, verses 17-21.
- As a whole class ask members to call out different images and phrases concerning Yahweh that they heard in the Scripture just read.
- Discuss the implications of the viewpoint of God as warrior for today's international relations.
—Is this biblical perspective helpful, or dangerous, in today's world?
—How is this warrior-God viewpoint similar to or different from your class members' understanding of God? If it is different, what facilitated the change of view?
- Following the discussion, you may want to ask the group to form a circle and to offer sentence prayers for peace, stability, and understanding among the nations and peoples of the world.

(I) Participate in a solemn ritual of contrition, prayer, and steadfast hope in God.

- In preparation for this ritual, you will need to photocopy the script for every member of the class.
- Set a table at the front of your classroom for a worship center. Place on the table several candles.
- Assign class members to one of three groups: group one will read the Leader's lines; group two will read the lines assigned to Respondents A; group three will read the lines assigned to Respondents B.

Leaders:
"Blow the trumpet in Zion;
    sanctify a fast;
call a solemn assembly;
    gather the people.
Sanctify the congregation;
    assemble the aged;
gather the children,
    even infants at the breast.
Let the bridegroom leave his room,
    and the bride her canopy."
                                    (Joel 2:15-16)

Respondents A:
"How long, O LORD? Will you be angry forever?
    Will your jealous wrath burn like fire?"
                                    (Psalm 79:5)
"Restore us again, O God of our salvation,
    and put away your indignation toward us.
Will you be angry with us forever?
    Will you prolong your anger to all generations?
Will you not revive us again,
    so that your people may rejoice in you?
Show us your steadfast love, O LORD,
    and grant us your salvation."
                                    (Psalm 85:4-7)

Respondents B:
"Turn, O LORD! How long?
    Have compassion on your servants!
Satisfy us in the morning with your steadfast love,
    so that we may rejoice and be glad all our day.
Make us glad as many days as you have afflicted us,
    and as many years as we have seen evil.
Let your work be manifest to your servants,
    and your glorious power to their children.
Let the favor of the Lord our God be upon us,
    and prosper for us the work of our hands—
    O prosper the work of our hands!"
                                    (Psalm 90:13-17)

Leaders:
"Happy are those whom you discipline, O LORD,
    and whom you teach out of your law,
giving them respite from days of trouble,
    until a pit is dug for the wicked.
For the LORD will not forsake his people;
    he will not abandon his heritage;
for justice will return to the righteous,
    and all the upright in heart will follow it."
                                    (Psalm 94:12-15)

From JOURNEY THROUGH THE BIBLE: EZEKIEL—MALACHI. Copyright © 1996 by Cokesbury. Permission is granted to photocopy this page.

Respondents A:
"O come, let us worship and bow down,
    let us kneel before the LORD, our Maker!
For he is our God,
    and we are the people of his pasture,
    and the sheep of his hand."
                                    (Psalm 95:6-7)

Respondents B:
"Truly the eye of the LORD is on those who fear him,
    on those who hope in his steadfast love,
to deliver their soul from death,
    and to keep them alive in famine."
                                    (Psalm 33:18-19)

Leaders:
"Our soul waits for the LORD;
    he is our help and shield.
Our heart is glad in him,
    because we trust in his holy name."
                                    (Psalm 33:20)

All:
"Let your steadfast love, O LORD, be upon us,
    even as we hope in you."
                                    (Psalm 33:22)

(J) Determine who is responsible for the care of creation.

If your class members have been interested in the discussion of the ecological disasters given in Joel, you may want to pursue the question of responsibility for creation. This learning option should help begin that discussion.

- If you have not already read Joel 1 aloud, do so. Invite different class members to read different sections of the chapter.
- Discuss their understanding of creation and who is responsible for caring for it. The following questions should get you started:

—According to the ancient Israelites, who is in total control of creation? Who brings the rain? Who sends the pests? (In our modern-day world this seems like the "simple life"; that is before humanity began abusing the gift of creation and before humanity began to understand how creation is ordered, the scientific principles that govern the world.)

—So, through the rain clouds and principles of evaporation and condensation, God does send the rain, but is God responsible for the quality of the rain?

—Perhaps we should don sackcloth and offer laments to God. But is that enough? What is a partnership with God for the care of creation like?

- In closing this discussion you may want to read from Chief Seattle's letter (circa 1852) to the United States government officials when the government wanted to buy the lands of the Suquamish and Duwamish Native Americans. (You can find this letter in Bill Moyers' book, with Joseph Campbell, *The Power of Myth* [Doubleday, 1988; pages 32–35], or an adaptation of the letter in Susan Jeffers' children's book, *Brother Eagle, Sister Sky*; Dial Books, 1991.)

Here are a few quotations:

"The President in Washington sends word that he wishes to buy our land. But how can you buy or sell the sky? The land? The idea is strange to us. If we do not own the freshness of the air and the sparkle of the water, how can you buy them?"

"Will you teach your children what we have taught our children? That the earth is our mother? What befalls the earth befalls all the sons [and daughters] of the earth."

"One thing we know: our god is also your god. The earth is precious to him [God] and to harm the earth is to heap contempt on its creator."

"We love this earth as a newborn loves its mother's heartbeat. So, if we sell you our land, love it as we have loved it. Care for it as we have cared for it. Hold in your mind the memory of the land as it is when you receive it. Preserve the land for all children and love it, as God loves us all."

K) Sing a hymn.

Joel 2:28-29 anticipates a time when the gifts of the spirit will be bestowed upon all humankind.
- Join in singing "Of All the Spirit's Gifts to Me," *The United Methodist Hymnal*, 336.
- If class members do not feel comfortable singing, ask them to read stanzas 1–4 responsively—perhaps men and women reading alternate stanzas; or divide into four groups, each group reading one stanza; or ask four readers to each read one stanza; or use another division that fits your group best—then ask all to join in reading stanza 5 together.

Additional Bible Helps

Prophecy and the Cult

In *A History of Prophecy in Israel*, biblical scholar Joseph Blenkinsopp speaks of cultic prophecy during the postexilic (Persian) period of Israel's history:

"One of the most important aspects of the transformation that prophecy underwent after the loss of national independence was its reabsorption into the cult [religious practices].

. . . .

"The change in the location and consequent understanding of prophecy is apparent in the early Persian period with the predominance of liturgical forms and cultic [religious] concerns in Haggai, Zechariah, Third Isaiah, and Malachi. It is also much in evidence in the address of a certain Joel ben-Pethuel to the congregation, which included farmers and vintners, on the occasion of a disastrous plague of locusts that had ruined the crops. . . .

"The opening address to the congregation (Joel 1:2-12) concludes with a call to the priests to convoke a solemn service of fasting and repentance (1:13-18) to which the people were summoned by the blowing of the shofar (2:1, 15). There follow the prayer of petition (1:19-20) and the call to fast and repent (2:1-17), and the liturgical action ends with an oracle of assurance delivered by the prophet (2:18-27). . . . [B]y the time of Joel there can be no doubt that the averting of disaster could be achieved, if at all, only by the cultic [religious] act of the entire community. For Joel, whose criticism of his contemporaries is mild in comparison with that of Amos (Joel 1:5; 2:12), the current threat to the economic existence of the community can be turned aside only by means of cultic [religious] acts performed in the Temple, in which the prophet played a leading role" (The Westminster Press, 1983; pages 252–54).

Historically, biblical scholars have exhibited something of a bias against religious prophecy, on the presumption that prophets affiliated with central establishment institutions (such as the royal court, the official religious personnel) felt constrained to speak oracles that would be favorable to the king, officiating priests, and so on. As Blenkinsopp notes, however, prophets played important roles in the postexilic cultus [religious life] (and likely in the preexilic ritual life of ancient Israel as well). Prejudice against such prophets, therefore, can distort our understanding of how prophecy—like all living phenomena—changed and developed over the course of its history in Israel.

For learning option (G) in the next lesson you will need a photocopy of the article on pages 68–70, "Messianic Motifs in the Book of the Twelve," for every class member.

13 "See, a Day Is Coming for The Lord"

Haggai; Zechariah; Malachi

LEARNING MENU
Keeping in mind the ways in which your class members learn best, as well as their needs and interests, choose at least one learning option from each of the three Dimensions.

Dimension 1: What Does the Bible Say?

(A) Begin with meditation and prayer.

- Prior to class, arrange for three persons to assume the roles of Leaders 1, 2, and 3. Each leader should have a copy of their part listed below. You may want to copy these off on note cards for these persons.
- Begin by inviting the class to sing or recite the words to the hymn "Holy Spirit, Truth Divine" (*The United Methodist Hymnal*, 465). Then ask the leaders to read their Scripture passages and prayers.

—**Leader 1:** Hear these words from the prophet Haggai: "Take courage, all you people . . . , says the LORD; . . . for I am with you, says the LORD of hosts. . . . My spirit abides among you; do not fear" (Haggai 2:4-5).
Prayer: Gracious God, as you were with your people in the days of Haggai, your prophet, empowering them by your spirit to rebuild your Temple, embolden us today as we work to extend the ministry of your church to a world torn by hunger and strife. Keep us mindful, as we minister to others, of our own needs and shortcomings. Amen.

—**Leader 2:** Hear these words from the prophet Zechariah: "This is the word of the LORD . . . : Not by might, nor by power, but by my spirit, says the LORD of hosts" (4:6).
Prayer: God of might and power, forgive us when we presuppose that we are able by our own strength to heal ourselves and others. Remind us that without your spirit, we labor in vain. Amen.

—**Leader 3:** Hear God's words through the prophet Zechariah: "I will save you and you shall be a blessing. Do not be afraid, but let your hands be strong. . . . These are the things that you shall do: Speak the truth to one another, render in your gates judgments that are true and make for peace, do not devise evil in your hearts against one another, and love no false oath; for all these are things that I hate, says the LORD" (8:13, 16-17).
Prayer: God of strength and blessing, strengthen our hands that we may in all things do your will. Empower us to speak the truth to one another, to be just and faithful. Kindle in our hearts the desire to be instruments of your love in our communities, our continent, and our world. Amen.

(B) Answer the questions in the study book.

● Discussion of Dimension 1 questions might include the following responses:

Haggai

1. According to Haggai 1:1-2, the prophet addresses Zerubbabel, a civil authority, and Joshua, the high priest. Hence, he speaks to the community's authorities. Yet "these people" and their failure to rebuild the Temple are the focus of his words. Because the community has seen to its own houses, but left Yahweh's house in ruins, thereby failing to honor their covenant obligation to God—all their efforts to provide for themselves have proven futile.

2. Haggai addresses those older members of the community who can remember when the magnificent Temple constructed during King Solomon's reign still stood in Jerusalem. (Perhaps their memories of the first Temple were even more glorious in retrospect!) Haggai acknowledges that the Temple now in process may appear "as nothing" to them (2:3). Yet he encourages Zerubbabel, Joshua, and all the people to trust in Yahweh's promise, and to be strengthened by God's spirit. For "in a little while," God declares, "I will shake the heavens and the earth and the sea and the dry land; and I will shake all the nations, so that the treasure of all nations shall come, and I will fill this house with splendor, says the LORD of Hosts. The silver is mine and the gold is mine" (2:6-8). Here, the author may have in mind the Temple vessels taken from the first Temple as booty by the Babylonians. Soon, Yahweh continues, the splendor of the second Temple will exceed that of the first, and the people will enjoy prosperity.

Zechariah

1. Yahweh urges those exiles remaining in Babylon to flee from the land of their captivity and return to Zion. Though in the past, God's judgment dispersed the people of Israel "like the four winds of heaven," now the Lord declares of the nations who have plundered them, "truly, one who touches you touches the apple [pupil] of my eye"—one of the most sensitive parts of the divine self. This anthropomorphic image is followed by another: "See now, I am going to raise my hand against them" (2:9). The Babylonians who plundered and enslaved others shall themselves be plundered by their slaves. Hence, daughter Zion is enjoined to sing and rejoice, for Yahweh shall dwell in her midst. Moreover, other nations also shall "join themselves to the LORD on that day, and shall be my people" (2:11). This universal statement is followed in verse 12 by a reassertion of Yahweh's particular relationship to Judah and Jerusalem.

Malachi

1. Yahweh charges that the priests are dishonoring God by sacrificing blind, lame, and sick animals to Yahweh as burnt offerings. Such offerings would never be accepted by a civil authority and so could not secure his favor. Neither shall they elicit God's graciousness. It would be better for the Temple doors to be shut than for such inferior offerings to be brought by those who promise to bring their best, yet cheat God.

2. According to Malachi 3:8-12, the postexilic community robs God when it fails to bring to the Temple the full tithe necessary for its maintenance. Yahweh invites those addressed to "put me to the test" (verse 10). If they fulfill their commitment to God, then they will receive God's blessings.

Dimension 2: What Does the Bible Mean?

(C) Engage in accusation and rebuttal.

● Provide paper and a pencil or pen for every two class members.
● Ask each pair to write a paraphrase of Haggai's rebuke of the postexilic community in Haggai 1:2-11.
● Ask participants to think creatively about how Haggai's audience—Zerubbabel and Joshua, as well as all the people—might have responded to his words. Recall that people tend to justify their actions, rather than admitting that charges lodged against them are true.
● When class members have completed these two tasks, ask them to share their findings with the class as a whole. Then discuss the following question:
—Do the responses you have written for the postexilic community bear any resemblance to discussions among your congregation members about the undertaking of new projects by your local church?

(D) Make a collage.

● Tape or tack pieces of posterboard or newsprint to a wall in your classroom until you have a surface approximately three feet by five feet.
● Provide class members with newspapers, news magazines, glue, scissors, and markers.
● Ask them to read Haggai 1:2-11 and then to make a collage depicting modern-day conditions similar to those pertaining to the postexilic community of Haggai's lifetime.
● Allow time for each "artist" to share the meaning of his or her contributions to the collage.

(E) Create a picture.

● Participants will need paper, colored pencils or pens, scissors, construction paper or tissue paper, and glue.
● Divide class members into eight groups. Each group will work with one of Zechariah's visions.

Group One—1:7-17
Group Two—1:18-21
Group Three—2:1-13
Group Four—3:1-10
Group Five—4:1-14
Group Six—5:1-4
Group Seven—5:5-11
Group Eight—6:1-8

- When the groups have finished reading, ask them to create a picture. This picture may be a symbol for the larger vision or it may be a representation of the figures in the vision itself.
- Recruit a spokesperson from each group to tell about the group's picture as well as the group's interpretation of the larger meaning of the vision.
—How does what they have produced communicate the principal ideas communicated in Zechariah's visions?

> **THE EIGHT VISIONS OF ZECHARIAH**
> 1. Horses and riders patrolling the earth (1:7-17)
> 2. Removal of international threats to the community (1:18-21)
> 3. Yahweh's presence in Jerusalem (chapter 2)
> 4. Purification of the priesthood (chapter 3)
> 5. Yahweh's guiding presence (chapter 4)
> 6. Removal of the curse from the community (5:1-4)
> 7. Removal of internal threats to the community (5:5-11)
> 8. Horses and chariots patrolling the earth (6:1-8)
>
> Note the correspondence between visions one and eight on the one hand, and visions two and seven on the other. The structure of the visions focuses attention especially on visions four and five, which speak to the religious practice of purification and to Yahweh's presence.

(F) Discuss the end of prophecy.

For many weeks or even months perhaps we have been studying the words of prophets. We have been reading, reflecting, and pondering the meaning from these ancient words. Now Zechariah reports that the prophetic words will cease.

- Before class time read the "Additional Bible Helps," page 66, and be prepared to include this information in your class discussion.
- Ask a class member to read aloud Zechariah 13:2-6. In these verses the prophet anticipates the end of prophecy in Israel.
- Discuss the following questions:
—What will parents do to children who prophesy?
—How shall prophets seek to disavow their association with prophesying? (Zechariah 13:2 begins with the phrase "on that day," suggesting conditions that will exist at an unknown time in the future. It first asserts that the "names of the idols" will be cut off from the land. Apparently, the postexilic community, like its preexilic predecessors, could still be enticed by the deities of other nations. But it goes further to promise the removal of prophets and "the unclean spirit" [the latter phrase appears nowhere else in Hebrew Scripture]. Subsequent verses assert that in the future, the parents of prophets will slay them as they prophesy. And even the prophets themselves will be ashamed of their visions, refusing to wear a "hairy mantle"—apparently a garment associated with prophetic activity—and asserting that the characteristic wounds on their chests were received "in the house of my friends".)
- Be sure to note to class members how in the Gospel of Luke (1:17) the ministry of John the Baptist marked the resumption of the prophetic inspiration in Israel.

(G) Read and discuss the essay, "Messianic Motifs in the Book of the Twelve."

> **TEACHING TIP**
> If you select this learning activity, you will need to make copies of the essay "Messianic Motifs in the Book of the Twelve" (pages 68-70 in this leader's guide) and make them available to class members prior to your session if possible.

- You or someone in the group should be prepared to summarize the essay briefly just before the discussion period.
- Ask volunteers to share their thoughts about this essay with the entire class.
- Then discuss with the whole class the following questions:
—How does awareness of the early Christians' use of ancient Israel's prophetic literature increase your knowledge of the New Testament?
—Does this essay cast a different light on Jesus' activity as described in the Gospels?
—How does the role of John the Baptist become richer taken in light of the Old Testament prophetic references?
—How does it contribute to your understanding of the early Christian debate concerning Gentile converts to Christianity?

Dimension 3: What Does the Bible Mean to Us?

(H) Reflect on the meaning of Zechariah 4:6.

- For this learning option you will need a large sheet of newsprint and markers or a chalkboard and chalk.
- Ask class members to sit comfortably, to close their eyes, and then to listen as a class member reads aloud the fourth

chapter of Zechariah. After the end of the reading allow a few quiet moments.
- According to Zechariah 4:6, the prophet's angelic intermediary conveys the following words from Yahweh to Zerubbabel: "Not by might, nor by power, but by my spirit, says the LORD of hosts."
- These words, though rooted to a particular person and situation in the Book of Zechariah, bear potential significance for all persons of faith.
- Roughly sketch out the vision scene—a seven-branched lampstand and an olive tree on each side.
- Discuss with class members what this vision may have meant for Zechariah's culture. During the course of the discussion you may want to clarify these points:
—The lamps are the "eyes of the LORD."
—The trees are the two anointed ones who stand by the Lord of the whole earth. These anointed ones are Zerubbabel, the ruler, and Joshua, the high priest.
—These two, Zerubbabel and Joshua are to rule jointly—the government of the land shall be not by might (secular ruler), nor by power (sacred priest), but by my (Yahweh's) spirit.
—Zechariah prophesies that both the government and the religious leadership need God's guidance to create together a just rule.
- You may want to ask this question:
—How does this speak to the United States's Constitution of separation of church and state?

(I) Find out what "covenant faithfulness" can mean for Christians today.

- Divide class members into three groups, supply them with paper and pens or pencils.

Part One:
- Ask each group to read Malachi 1:6-9; 2:10-11; and 3:8-10.
- Ask these questions of each group:
—How was the priesthood corrupt? (1:6-9)
—How has Judah proven itself a faithless covenant partner to Yahweh (2:10-11)? (Judah has proven a faithless covenant partner because it has profaned Yahweh's sanctuary and "married the daughter of a foreign god"—gave reverence to the goddess Asherah. Here, the prophet uses marriage imagery to describe how Judah (here, the husband) has turned away from Yahweh (here depicted as the wife).
—How have the offerings been at the Temple? (3:8-10)

Part Two:
- Now with a better understanding of the "covenant faithfulness" addressed by Malachi, how are *we* doing?

—What does "covenant faithfulness" mean for us?
—In what ways has our congregation demonstrated its covenant faithfulness to God?
—What problems and competing loyalties test our resolve to be faithful covenant partners with God?
- Ask each small group to write a prayer or a responsive reading about their congregation's covenant faithfulness to God.
- At the end of ten minutes, ask a representative to read the group's prayer.

(J) Select a verse to carry with you.

- Divide class members into conversation groups of three persons each. Supply each person with slips of paper and a pen or pencil.
- Ask the members of each group, in dialogue with one another, to select a passage from Haggai, Zechariah, or Malachi that they would like to carry with them in their wallet or in their Bible during the coming week. Each person can then write this verse on a slip of paper.
- Persons may wish to explain to others in their group the significance of the passage they have chosen.

(K) Celebrate the joy of being in God's presence!

In Psalm 84, an ancient Israelite poet expresses the love and joy he experiences in the presence of Yahweh's Temple. This will make a nice closing not only for this lesson but for the entire study on the Prophets.
- A responsive reading on Psalm 84 appears on pages 804-805 in *The United Methodist Hymnal*. If your class enjoys singing try singing the response.
- Divide class members into two groups. Group one should read those verses printed in regular type. Group two should read the verses printed in bold type. The entire class should join in singing or reciting the response (R).

Additional Bible Helps

Zechariah 13:2-6 and the End of Prophecy in Israel
From the outset, we have noted that prophecy was a problematic institution in ancient Israel for many reasons. First, prophecy did not exist in a vacuum. Ancient Israel's prophets and their oracles were inevitably influenced by a vast array of factors—political, economical, historical, and theological. As a result, god-fearing intermediaries addressing issues from varying perspectives could and did disagree with one another.

Second, no single criterion sufficed in every situation for distinguishing between an authentic intermediary between Yahweh and the human community and a false intermediary. Deuteronomy 18:21-22, for example, stipulated that the people should not believe a prophet whose prediction was not fulfilled. But this test was not applicable to nonpredictive prophecies (of which there were many) and required the advantage of hindsight.

Third, prophets no less than other persons within ancient Israelite society could be lured into taking bribes, or tempted to say the "right things" to people in positions of power. Both central prophets (who functioned within established power structures and worked to bring about orderly and positive changes within those structures) and peripheral prophets (who functioned outside the establishment and advocated an overthrow of the status quo) could be influenced by their support communities.

Fourth, during times of apocalyptic fervor, when people hoped for God's imminent and dramatic intervention in history, prophets sometimes stirred up rebellion, inciting zealots to dangerous acts. When expectations failed to materialize, people paid the price for their rash actions.

For these and other reasons, the view emerged during the postexilic period that prophetic inspiration had ceased in Israel and would only resume at some time in the future (Joel 2:28-29; Malachi 4:5). Zechariah 13:2-6 contains a strongly worded statement against those who continue to engage in activities associated with at least some types of prophecy. According to 13:3, parents who catch their children acting as prophets may inflict capital punishment upon them, without first bringing that child before the community's elders for communal judgment (see also Deuteronomy 21:18-21).

Moreover, those who have worn the attire characteristic of prophets, and whose bodies bear the marks of their profession, will disavow their prophetic vocation and be ashamed of their visions. Verse 5 quotes them as saying, "I am no prophet, I am a tiller of the soil; for the land has been my possession since my youth"—words that echo Amos's denial to Amaziah, the priest, that he was a professional prophet (Amos 7:14).

For Luke, the ministry of John the Baptist (identified with the Elijah prophecy of Malachi 4:5) marked the resumption of prophetic inspiration in Israel (Luke 1:17).

Messianic Motifs in the Book of the Twelve

By John A. Darr

Introduction: Early Christian Defense

The primary difficulty facing early Christians was how to argue for both continuity and discontinuity, for Jesus' coherence with prior Jewish tradition, and his apparent difference from much of it. How could the Messiah be both the "son of David" (with all the military and political implications of that title) and nonviolent; triumphant but suffering and dying; magnificent yet humble; a stern judge and a peacemaker; accepted and rejected; for Jews but also for Gentiles? The early Christians believed that the connection between what God had done with Israel and what God had done in Jesus (and was still doing among them) was essential. But how were they to explain and solidify that connection in the face of seeming incongruities? In many ways, Jesus simply did not fufill popular Jewish messianic expectations; and the early Christians were doing and saying things that seemed tremendously at odds with tradition. This difficult task found much support in certain passages found in the so-called minor prophets. In short, the minor prophets were a major aid to the Christians.

This brief essay is not the place to catalog all the instances in which New Testament authors drew upon the minor prophets. Instead, I shall discuss three major ways in which these ancient traditions contributed to the early Christians' overall defense of Jesus as Messiah.

A New Era, a New Way, a New Revelation

One of the main strategies the Christians used to validate the newness of their ideas and way of life was to claim that a new age had dawned and that this new era had been predicted in Scripture. In other words, what other Jews perceived as clear breaks with Jewish tradition by the followers of Jesus were actually anticipated (so the Christians argued) within that tradition. Different religious ideas were to be expected in the climactic end times when God stepped into history directly and delivered a new revelation on earth. The old rules no longer applied, at least not in the same ways.

The minor prophets, along with major exilic and postexilic prophets, were especially useful in this kind of argument, for they too had spoken of a new age of hope when God would pour out the Spirit upon the earth, redeem the people from exile, write a new law on their hearts, and reconstitute the Temple, the liturgy, and the priesthood. Prophecy would bloom once more. The dramatic decisiveness of this salvation-orientated shift is hauntingly expressed in words the prophet Joel attributes to Yahweh:

> "Then afterward
> I will pour out my spirit on all flesh;
> your sons and your daughters shall prophesy,
> your old men shall dream dreams,
> and your young men shall see visions."
> (Joel 2:28; see Acts 2:17-18)

The early Christians felt that they were living in the "afterward" of Joel's oracle, in the critical period of salvation history, a time full of new possibilities and a permanently altered relationship with God.

But what evidence did the Christians have that a new age had indeed been inaugurated? One of their main proofs was the advent of the "preparer of the way of the Lord," predicted in various ways by several of the prophets. In Christian thought, both John and Jesus exemplified aspects of this marvelous eschatological (theological thought concerned with the end of history) figure. It is hardly coincidental that believers in Jesus (unlike other Jews) arranged their canon of Scripture to end climactically with God's words in Malachi 4:5:

> "Lo, I will send you the prophet Elijah before the great and terrible day of the Lord comes. He will turn the hearts of parents to their children and the hearts of children to their parents, so that I will not come and strike the land with a curse."

This sets the stage directly for the advent of John the Baptist and Jesus. In Luke 1:17, the angel of the Lord informs Zechariah that his son, John, will play Elijah's role and thus fulfill Malachi's prophecy:

> "With the spirit and power of Elijah he will go before

From Journey Through the Bible: Ezekiel—Malachi. Copyright © 1996 by Cokesbury. Permission is granted to photocopy this page.

him, to turn the hearts of parents to their children, and the disobedient to the wisdom of the righteous, to make ready a people prepared for the Lord."

As Luke (and many other believers) construed salvation history, John functioned as the returning Elijah and indeed as the representative of the prophetic voice and message. He proclaimed the coming of the Lord (although in Luke this is nonspecific in terms of person and time), but his main task was the preparation of hearts. Without John's "baptism of repentance for the forgiveness of sins," people would not be able to see and experience the "salvation of the Lord" when it appeared. John called for a radical change of attitude, a turning away from social and spiritual injustice and abuse (see Luke 3:7-18); in other words, Luke's John distilled the moral and ethical teaching of the ancient prophets and this set the stage for the appearance of Jesus as the Lord.

In neither the prophets nor the New Testament is the coming of the Lord considered all sweetness and light. It is, rather, a time of testing, trial, cleansing, refining, and reconstruction. It brings salvation on the one hand and a fire that consumes and purifies on the other. Jesus' cleansing of the Temple functioned in the latter sense for the early Christians. Once again, Malachi provided an important intertextual link for this christological (doctrine based on the belief in Christ) interpretation:

"See, I am sending my messenger to prepare the way before me, and the Lord whom you seek will suddenly *come to his temple*. The messenger of the covenant in whom you delight—indeed, he is coming, says the LORD of hosts. But who can endure the day of his coming, and who can stand when he appears?

"For he is like a refiner's fire and like fullers' soap; he will sit as a refiner and purifier of silver, and he will purify the descendants of Levi and refine them like gold and silver, until they present offerings to the LORD in righteousness."
(Malachi 3:1-3, italics added)

Jesus' dramatic words and actions among the moneychangers and traders in the Temple gained further significance when viewed in light of the last verse of Zechariah, another minor prophet: "And there shall no longer be traders in the house of the LORD of hosts on that day" (14:21b; see John 2:16). In light of these oracles, Jesus' conflicts with the priesthood and other aspects of the current religious practice were justified to Jews who revered the Temple as the central institution of Judaism.

It should be added that the prophetic idea of the "way of the Lord" was appropriated by the early Christians to describe the experience of following Jesus. The Synoptic evangelists (Matthew, Mark, and Luke) rely heavily on the journey motif (Jesus and his disciples "on the way") in their retellings of the gospel story. Jesus' climactic trip to Jerusalem thus has less to do with geographical moves than with the spiritual journey his followers make as they seek to understand and respond to him (see Mark 8:27–10:52). From this perspective, the "way" that is to be prepared is not topographical (leveling mountains), or primarily sociological (eliminating class distinctions), but within the heart and experience of those yearning to believe. And, of course, the way is not easy, or glorious, or triumphant, but one that leads to opposition, rejection, suffering, and death. Mark's Jesus warns his followers:

"As for yourselves, beware; for they will hand you over to councils; and you will be beaten in synagogues; and you will stand before governors and kings because of me, as a testimony to them."
(Mark 13:9)

A Suffering, Humble, Peaceful Messiah

The "way" that John the Baptist and Jesus both prepared and trod was difficult to follow and to convince other Jews to follow. Was not the Messiah meant to deliver us from suffering, rather than to call us to still more trials and humiliation? How can we believe in a "messiah" who was opposed by our leadership and who died a demeaning death on a Roman cross? The early Christian defense for this tragic aspect of their sacred story depended heavily on Zechariah. In predicting Peter's denial of him (and the other disciples' desertion of him), Jesus echoes haunting imagery from this ancient text: "You will all become deserters; for it is written, 'I will strike the shepherd, and the sheep will be scattered' " (Mark 14:27; from Zechariah 13:7b). The shepherd, of course, was a common metaphor for the king (anointed one, messiah); and this passage had originally referred to a king of Judah who was to fall (or had fallen) in battle. The sheep, then, referred to the Lord's people. As put on the lips of Jesus, this prophecy supported the notion that the messiah was to die, and that his followers were to be somewhat in disarray for a period following his death.

Other royal imagery in Zechariah helped the early Christians explain discrete aspects of Jesus' actions, attitudes, and experiences, especially during his final week in Jerusalem. All four of the Gospels record the "triumphal entry," which can only be called triumphal with the help of a strong dose of irony. How can the mood be victorious and yet so subdued? How can the procession be triumphal and yet lead to death? How can the same crowds that hail Jesus on this occasion call for his execution a few days later? The early Christians found a theological rationale for these issues in the strikingly paradoxical imagery of Zechariah 9:9-10, which is quoted and/or alluded to in all the Gospel accounts:

"Rejoice greatly, O daughter Zion!
  Shout aloud, O daughter Jerusalem!
Lo, your king comes to you;
  triumphant and victorious is he,
humble and riding on a donkey,
  on a colt, the foal of a donkey."

From JOURNEY THROUGH THE BIBLE: EZEKIEL—MALACHI. Copyright © 1996 by Cokesbury. Permission is granted to photocopy this page.

Jesus' symbolic actions (almost all scholars agree that a historical incident lies behind this story) derive their sacred depth and resonance from this scriptural quotation. He is both kingly (messianic) and humble, powerful and peaceful (see verse 10). Thus the scriptural tradition can support the notion of a nonmilitaristic, unspectacular Savior for Israel and the nations, a Messiah who exercises dominion not through force, but rather, through humility and peacefulness.

Besides the scattering of the sheep and triumphal entry traditions, several other passages from Zechariah helped the early Christians flesh out a defense for Jesus' suffering and death. First, Zechariah 9:11 ("because of the *blood of my covenant* with you, / I will set your prisoners free from the waterless pit" [italics added]) echoes in our earliest Communion formula: "This cup is the new covenant in my blood" (1 Corinthians 11:25b). Second, the piercing of Jesus on the cross and the subsequent regret of the people of Jerusalem, are prefigured in Zechariah 12:10: "And I will pour out a spirit of compassion and supplication on the house of David and the inhabitants of Jerusalem, so that, *when they look on the one whom they have pierced*, they shall mourn for him, as one mourns for an only child, and weep bitterly over him, as one weeps over a firstborn" (italics added; see Matthew 24:30; John 19:37; and Revelation 1:7). Finally, Judas's "selling" of Jesus for thirty pieces of silver finds certain resonances in the bitter sarcasm of Zechariah 11:12-13 ("thirty shekels of silver . . . this lordly price at which I was valued by them").

Universal Salvation
One of the most heated controversies within early Christianity itself, and between Christians and non-Christian Jews, concerned the membership, participation, and role of Gentiles (non-Jews) within the chosen people of God. Non-Christian Jews and some conservative Jewish Christians felt that a strict distinction should be maintained between Jews and Gentiles, with the latter playing a strictly subordinate role in God's plan. Only full conversion to Judaism (including circumcision for males) and adherence to Torah would guarantee Gentiles a place among the elect (see Acts 15). But the internal logic of the Christians' argument for a new era of salvation, as well as the practical experience of witnessing so many Gentiles clamoring to belong to the new movement, pushed most Christian Jews to affirm that Gentiles who believed in Jesus were now to be considered part of the people of God with few, if any, conditions attached. Their argument for the inclusion of the Gentiles owed much to the prophets, who had often affirmed that Yahweh was the God of "the nations" as well as of Israel, and that God's historical plan included the Gentiles. The new age of revelation initiated by Jesus had eliminated the need for distinctions between Jew and Gentile in the sight of God. Had not Joel's oracle claimed that "afterward I will pour out my spirit on *all flesh*" (Joel 2:28, italics added; see also Zechariah 8:20-23)?

The greatest advocate of "Gentile rights" within the early church was the apostle Paul. He argued strenuously that Gentile believers need not be circumcised, follow the Jewish calendar, or heed the Jewish dietary laws, to be considered fully part of the people of God. Indeed, requiring Gentiles to obey the law, Paul argued, implicitly denied that God's revelation in Jesus was sufficient to save. Not the law but faith, not the letter but the spirit, not works but grace, were required for the salvation of Gentiles. To buttress this line of argumentation, Paul turned to Habakkuk (among other Scriptures):

"Then the LORD answered me and said:
Write the vision;
    make it plain on tablets,
    so that a runner may read it.
For there is still a vision for the appointed time;
    it speaks of the end, and does not lie.
If it seems to tarry, wait for it;
    it will surely come, it will not delay.
Look at the proud!
    Their spirit is not right in them,
    but the righteous shall live by their faith."
(Habakkuk 2:2-4, italics added)

In Romans and Galatians, where Paul argues most vehemently for Gentile inclusion without legal constraint, he turns to the Habakkuk passage at crucial points: "Now it is evident that no one is justified before God by the law; for 'The one who is righteous will live by faith' " (Galatians 3:11; Romans 1:16-17). Paul thus uses the prophetic message of the primacy of interiority (heart attitude) over exteriority (ceremony, status, and legal observation) to defend the validity of Gentile conversions without the imposition of Jewish law.

Conclusion
Early Christian theologians were not interested in historical-critical interpretations of the minor prophets. In their original settings, these oracles had dealt with current (or imminent) events and personages, with actual kings and historical circumstances in the sixth through the second centuries B.C. In good midrashic (midrash was a form of Jewish scriptural interpretation) fashion, however, the early church drew selectively on these prophecies to explain, expand, and defend their understanding of Jesus as Messiah and the lifestyle and community engendered by that understanding.

Watching in the Night Visions:
Daniel's Apocalypse and Early Christian Reflection on Jesus

By John A. Darr

Introduction
Most modern Christians are not used to thinking of early Christianity as a diverse, developing, changing, and theologically creative movement. We need, therefore, to take a closer look at some of the terms and to explain social and historical circumstances that shed light on our beginnings.

Apocalyptic (pertaining to a prophetic disclosure or revelation) writings provided an important overall worldview for the church's first theologians. And Daniel's apocalyptic vision was very influential in the thought of the early church, especially his vivid imagery of a mysterious "son of man."

"I saw in the night visions,
and behold, with the clouds of heaven
there came one like a son of man,
and he came to the Ancient of Days
and was presented before him.
And to him was given dominion
and glory and kingdom,
that all peoples, nations, and languages
should serve him;
his dominion is an everlasting dominion,
which shall not pass away,
and his kingdom one
that shall not be destroyed."
(Daniel 7:13-14, Revised Standard Version)

As early believers in Jesus (and perhaps Jesus himself) reflected on Jesus' identity and significance, this passage became a touchstone for their deliberations. To their way of thinking, Jesus must have been, or in the near future would be revealed as, this "son of man."

Apocalyptic
All the Abrahamic religions (Judaism, Christianity, and Islam) include strains of apocalyptic within their traditions. Although apocalyptic is hardly the dominant mode for any of these religions, it enjoys periodic resurgences among certain of their adherents. The basic characteristics of such movements are clearly recognizable. The apocalyptic outlook is heavily dominated by *eschatology*, teaching concerning the end of history. Members of apocalyptic movements believe that God has revealed secret information about the imminent end of the world to their leader. The revelation usually takes the form of a vivid, dramatic, and highly symbolic vision that is interpreted by a heavenly figure and then written down and transmitted to members of the in-group by the *seer*, the leader who experiences the vision. Hence, what binds the group together and distinguishes it from others is possession of special knowledge concerning how history will culminate. The Branch Davidians are a good example of a recently generated Christian apocalyptic sect.

The apocalyptic worldview is at one and the same time full of despair and hope: despair that the current world order will ever be righteous and just, but hope that God will ultimately intervene and restore the world to pristine condition. Members of such groups are convinced that the world is spiralling downward to catastrophe. Political, social, and religious programs cannot stop this tragic slide into chaos and destruction. Liberals and other progressive types make poor apocalypticists; and, indeed, one does not find them in the pews of apocalyptic churches. Neither does one find rich and established folks here. The poor, the marginalized, the outcasts, the persecuted, the downtrodden—these are the ones who swell the ranks of apocalyptic communities. Their eschatologically oriented theology speaks to the issue of their treatment and lowly status in society: a great reversal will take place, for when God acts decisively, they will be justified, glorified, and placed in positions of power, whereas those who abuse them will be condemned and humiliated.

Jewish and Christian Apocalyptic
The roots of Jewish apocalyptic are notoriously difficult to trace. Such prophetic predictions were often made with the use of a wide palette of vivid metaphors and may be seen as predecessors of the highly symbolic and frequently disturbing "visions" of the apocalyptic seers. Furthermore, the prophetic warning that injustices to the poor and downtrodden were often the cause of imminent catastrophes to the nation must have resonated among the apocalypticists. Scholars have also identified elements of biblical wisdom literature, Babylonian astrology, and ancient Persian religion in Jewish apocalyptic.

From JOURNEY THROUGH THE BIBLE: EZEKIEL—MALACHI. Copyright © 1996 by Cokesbury. Permission is granted to photocopy this page.

All of these factors—prophecy, wisdom, astrology, and Persian religion—seem to have come into focus in the early to mid-second century B.C., a time of intense persecution of the Jews by their Hellenistic overlords. The latter were heirs of Alexander the Great's empire, which had been established over a century earlier. Alexander had conceived of his campaign as both political and cultural; not only did he seek to conquer territory, but he also wished to spread Greek language, philosophy, education, religion, art, and sport over the entire known world. Under intense cultural and military pressure, first from the Greeks and then from the Romans, many Jews turned to apocalyptic. They looked for savior figures, or "messiahs," to help them throw off the yoke of foreign domination and to reclaim and purify their religious institutions. The heyday of Jewish apocalyptic stretched from the second century B.C. through the early second century A.D. Many Jewish apocalyptic texts were written and revered; Daniel was the only one finally allowed into the Jewish canon.

Christianity began as a charismatic, apocalyptic sect within pre-A.D. 70 Judaism. The evidence for this claim is found in the earliest levels of Christian tradition, that is, in the oral traditions and written sources that underlie the Synoptic Gospels (Matthew, Mark and Luke), and in First Thessalonians, Paul's first letter, which was written perhaps as early as the mid-forties. Both "Q" (a sayings source underlying Matthew and Luke) and Mark (also used by Matthew and Luke) are highly apocalyptic in nature and rely heavily on the son of man imagery from Daniel in their presentations of Jesus. These early materials suggest strongly that the first Christians were marginalized Jews who formed prophetic communities and looked for the imminent return of Jesus as the apocalyptic son of man. As Christianity continued to evolve and institutionalize (develop offices, creeds, and canon), apocalyptic was stressed less and less by the emerging movement. By the second generation, many believers had already begun to think that Jesus' coming had been indefinitely postponed while the church established itself and evangelized the entire world. The consequences of this new eschatological outlook were predictable: apocalyptic fervor waned in favor of missionary zeal, bureaucratic development, and the achievement of status as a legitimate religion within the Roman Empire. Still, there were periodic resurgences of apocalyptic whenever crises arose and believers were persecuted. The Book of Revelation, our only thoroughly apocalyptic book in the New Testament, was probably written during one such period of wide-scale persecution of Christians in the late first century. All apocalyptic Scriptures are linked by a common dependence on Daniel as their primary scriptural source.

Daniel, Jesus, and the Early Church

Let's look now at that tantalizing Danielic phrase, "son of man" (in the New Revised Standard Version, "a human being"), a title that was applied to Jesus very early on in what may well have been the first attempt at christology (theological explanation of Jesus' nature, function, and significance).

First, however, a few words are in order concerning the role of the historical Jesus in all this apocalyptic theologizing. Was Jesus an apocalypticist? Scholars are divided over whether, or to what extent, Jesus himself intentionally drew on the son of man traditions from Daniel 7. Furthermore, those who believe that Jesus referred to this apocalyptic figure disagree as to whether Jesus identified himself with Daniel's son of man or whether Jesus' sayings about the son of man referred to another person. This is very probably one of those ultimately insoluble issues that biblical critics love to debate. Quite likely Jesus used apocalyptic ideas and alluded to Daniel's son of man; there can be no doubt, however, that soon after his death and resurrection, his followers identified him as *the* son of man and developed a complex apocalyptic christology around this imagery.

There seems to have been three dimensions to early Christian reflection on Jesus as the son of man:

● First are the *future* son of man sayings. These refer to the advent of the son of man and to his powers and activities when he arrives at some point in the future. Matthew 16:27-28 and Mark 13:26-27 are examples of this futuristic view.

The imagery of clouds and angels (Mark 13:26-27) comes directly from Daniel. What is new is the early Christian idea that Jesus will be the one to make this glorious appearance at his (second) coming. His tasks will be to gather the elect—the believers—and to judge the wicked.

● A second type of saying regarding the son of man *referred to and explained* Jesus' suffering, death, and resurrection. (See Matthew 17:22-23.)

This kind of saying is more difficult to tie directly to Daniel 7 and so should be seen as an early Christian expansion of the son of man idea to allow for the facts of Jesus' passion. From the perspective of believers, Jesus' vindication was provided by his resurrection, his exaltation to "the right hand of Power" (see Psalm 110:1), and his future return on the clouds of heaven. The same person who died such a dishonorable death would one day judge the world.

● Finally, there are the *present* son of man sayings, which express the authority of Jesus in his earthly ministry (see Matthew 12:8). The early Christians attributed the powers of the heavenly son of man to the earthly Jesus, as well as to the heavenly Jesus who would come in glory at a later time. Already in his ministry among them, Jesus had evidenced the authority and dominion promised to Daniel's son of man.

In conclusion, our short survey of early Christian apocalyptic has provided a window on some of the very first and most important theological reflection by believers in Jesus. That window reveals that our ancestors in the faith came to understand themselves and their Lord in large measure by "watching in the night visions" with Daniel.

From JOURNEY THROUGH THE BIBLE: EZEKIEL—MALACHI. Copyright © 1996 by Cokesbury. Permission is granted to photocopy this page.

(See map of Palestine on page 67).

Made in United States
Orlando, FL
25 April 2024